NEWSROOM CONFIDENTIAL

NEWSROOM CONFIDENTIAL

Lessons (and Worries) from an Ink-Stained Life

MARGARET SULLIVAN

ST. MARTIN'S PRESS
NEW YORK

First published in the United States by St. Martin's Press,
an imprint of St. Martin's Publishing Group

www.stmartins.com

Designed by Steven Seighman

Library of Congress Cataloging-in-Publication Data

Names: Sullivan, Margaret, 1957– author.
Title: Newsroom confidential : lessons (and worries) from an ink-stained life / Margaret Sullivan.
Description: First edition. | New York : St. Martin's Press, 2022. |
Identifiers: LCCN 2022020121 | ISBN 9781250281906 (hardcover) | ISBN 9781250281913 (ebook)
Subjects: LCSH: Sullivan, Margaret, 1957– | New York times—History. | Washington post—History. | Women journalists—United States—Biography. | Journalism—United States—History.
Classification: LCC PN4874.S779 A3 2022 | DDC 070.92 [B]—dc23/eng/20220705
LC record available at https://lccn.loc.gov/2022020121

First Edition: 2022

10 9 8 7 6 5 4 3 2 1

In memory of my parents, Jack and Elaine Sullivan,
with love and gratitude

Contents

Author's Note

Sections of this book describe my experiences at *The New York Times* and *The Washington Post,* where I was writing blog posts and columns at a rapid clip, sometimes as often as three or four times a week. I draw on those published pieces here, sometimes by directly quoting from them and sometimes by summarizing or paraphrasing. I also rely on the scores of journals I have kept for more than five decades—starting at age ten, when my father handed me a blank 1968 datebook that I decided to use as a diary.

NEWSROOM CONFIDENTIAL

Prologue

On January 6, 2021, the Covid pandemic was still raging, and amid the lockdown, it had been months since I had set foot in the *Washington Post* newsroom or covered a story in person. That once bustling D.C. newsroom was largely shuttered, along with the smaller New York City office where I often worked, and most of us—reporters, editors, and columnists—were working from home. Like almost everyone else, I watched Donald Trump's "Stop the Steal" rally, and the horrifying riot at the Capitol that followed, on TV. What started out looking like just another raucous rally turned downright frightening as a violent mob stormed the barricades. Even though I was safe at home, I could easily imagine myself there because both the Ellipse, near the White House, and the Capitol were less than a mile from where I had lived as Trump's presidency began. And I know what I saw: one of the most appalling moments in all of American history. Unlike the attacks on 9/11, decades earlier, this was an attack from within—incited by a defeated president who demanded that his vice president, Mike Pence, do what should have been unthinkable in the world's greatest democracy: reverse the results of a legitimate presidential election and give the loser an unearned second term.

The news coverage, of course, was wall-to-wall, even on Trump's favorite and most dependably supportive outlets, Fox News and One America News. You couldn't live in America and fail to understand what was happening. But it didn't take long for denialism to take hold. On that very day, at the pro-Trump network One America News, a supervisor reportedly ordered his staff to ignore the obvious: "Please DO NOT say 'Trump Supporters Storm Capitol.' . . . DO NOT CALL IT A RIOT!!!" By the spring, a Republican congressman would describe the violent attack as something that looked like a "normal tourist visit." By October, even the former vice president was trying to sow doubt. The rioters may have been chanting "Hang Mike Pence!" and they may have erected a symbolic gallows, but when Sean Hannity interviewed Pence on Fox News, the vice president downplayed the insurrection as merely "one day in January." He accused the mainstream media of giving it too much attention and of trying to demean Trump supporters.

This revisionism is working. As I write this, many months later, public opinion polls continue to reflect the nation's ugly divide and the refusal of many Americans to accept reality. Most Republicans believe—or *say* they believe—that the election was stolen from Trump. They believe this despite the lack of evidence and against the outcome of every court challenge and every politicized "audit" of votes in states like Pennsylvania and Arizona. They believe it, in large part, because of the constant drumbeat from right-wing media: on Fox, on podcasts, on radio shows, all amplified enormously on social media, especially on Facebook.

The traditional media—what I call the reality-based press—was at fault, too, in creating this democracy-threatening mess. In a less obvious way, they worsened the harm. They did so by treating the denialists as legitimate news sources whose views, for the sake of objectivity and fairness, must be respectfully listened to and reflected in news stories. By inviting the members of Congress's "insurrection caucus" on the Sunday broadcast-TV talk shows week after week. By framing the consequential decisions being made in Congress, including Trump's second impeachment, as just another lap in the horse race of politics. Examples abounded. When House Speaker Nancy Pelosi, quite reasonably, refused to give seats on an investigative committee to two congressmen who had backed Trump's efforts to invalidate the election, many journalists framed it as a partisan feud, not as an effort to protect the integrity of the committee. Politico even called Pelosi's necessary decision a "gift" to Kevin McCarthy, the Republican minority leader of the House of Representatives, again depicting the investigation as little but a political game, complete with winners and losers.

The extreme right wing had its staunch, all-in media allies; the rest of the country had a mainstream press that too often couldn't, or wouldn't, do their jobs. Too many journalists couldn't seem to grasp their crucial role in American democracy. Almost pathologically, they normalized the abnormal and sensationalized the mundane.

These days, we can clearly see the fallout from decades of declining public trust, the result, at least partly, of so many years of the press being undermined and of undermining itself. What is that fallout? Americans no longer share a common basis of reality. That's dangerous because American democracy, government by the people, simply can't function this way. It's high time to ask how public trust in the press steadily plummeted from the years following the Watergate scandal and the publication of the Pentagon Papers in the 1970s—when seven of ten Americans trusted the news—to today's rock-bottom lows.

For me, this story of lost trust is personal. I was drawn into journalism as a teenager, partly by the intrepid and history-changing Watergate reporting at *The Washington Post.* Soon after, I became the editor of my high school's student newspaper. After part-time clerking jobs and reporting for college newspapers, my career began for real. Over more than four decades, I've worked at news outlets as tiny as the *Niagara Gazette,* with its handful of reporters covering a small Western New York city, and as large as *The New York Times,* with nearly two thousand journalists posted all over the world.

As a young reporter, I nearly choked on the smoke and fumes as I covered a propane explosion in downtown Buffalo that took the lives of five firefighters and two civilians. Years later, as the newly minted chief editor of my hometown *Buffalo News,* I raced up to a standing microphone in a packed Washington, D.C., hotel ballroom and asked President Clinton a question that infuriated him; his answer made front-page news all over the country.

On September 11, 2001, I approved the 120-point headline on an emergency "extra" edition of the *News* that hit Buffalo's streets just hours after the terrorist attack in our state. As the public editor of *The New York Times,* I watched from a balcony overlooking the vast newsroom as publisher Arthur Sulzberger stunned the gathered staff by announcing that he had summarily replaced the paper's first woman editor, Jill Abramson, with its first Black editor, Dean Baquet.

I thought I had seen a lot in my career, but I wasn't prepared for the ugliness that came next. As a just-hired columnist for *The Washington Post,* I stood inside the Cleveland arena where Donald Trump was about to become the Republican nominee for president and heard the raucous crowd shouting out vitriol against Hillary Clinton—"Lock her up! Lock her up!" Two years later, I was taking notes in a packed Senate chamber as Facebook founder Mark Zuckerberg testified before Congress for the first time, with empty apologies for his company's endless misdeeds, including the ones that spread lies and helped Trump get elected. His presidency would have as a central theme the disparagement of the reality-based press, and a bizarre symbiosis with the right-wing media. For many Americans, that constant drumbeat would erode still further their already diminished trust in journalism and would heighten their antipathy toward reporters.

Journalism has been my profession, my obsession, and—maybe more than has been strictly wise—my life's focus. I believe in the power, the absolute necessity, of good reporting. I've admired it at its best, as journalism uncovers wrongdoing and illuminates the best and the worst of our society. Journalism matters—immensely—when it sends serial molesters, like the former USA Gymnastics doctor Larry Nassar, to jail; when it uncovers the criminal insider trading of a local congressman; when it points out abuses at a U.S. Army hospital; when it shows how poor pilot training can crash airplanes; when it proves how Facebook maximizes profit over truth. Journalism matters, too, when it spotlights great music, theater, and art or shows us inspiring examples of human courage. We need journalism—and we need it to be at its best, to be believed, and to *deserve* to be believed.

Much as I love and value my craft, I'm worried. I am sickened at the damage done by the hyperpartisan media and distressed about the failures of the reality-based press. We're in deep trouble. How did we Americans become trapped in this thicket of lies, mistrust, and division? Can we slash our way out? I believe we can, and must, but first let's see how we got here. My journey is personal, of course, *and* it tells the larger tale. Won't you come along? It starts in a steel town along the shore of Lake Erie, just south of Buffalo.

1

The Long Arm of Watergate

At twilight, the sky over Lackawanna would glow electric coral, but we kids were savvy enough to know that this spectacle was no gorgeous sunset over Lake Erie. It meant, to use the neighborhood slang, that "they dumped the slag at the plant." The plant was Bethlehem Steel, the hulking factory covering more than thirteen hundred acres along the shoreline just south of Buffalo; the slag was the molten industrial waste that was poured nightly out of huge vats onto the shoreline or right into the lake. We took this environmental travesty for granted as another daily ritual—like fetching the morning newspaper, the *Buffalo Courier-Express,* from the side door, and, some eight hours later, doing the same with *The Buffalo Evening News.*

Just as we believed in steelmaking as a community good—union wages, after all, for more than twenty thousand workers who didn't need a second income to support a family—we believed what appeared on those front pages. All the explosive issues of the day came to us that way: the Vietnam War, second-wave feminism, civil rights protests, the assassinations of John and Robert Kennedy and Dr. Martin Luther

King, Jr., and the deadly National Guard shootings of student protesters at Kent State University. My whole family read the papers, and like many of our neighbors, we watched the nightly CBS newscast anchored by "the most trusted man in America," Walter Cronkite, whose pessimistic appraisal of the Vietnam War in 1968 dealt a death blow to the American government's decades-long involvement. ("It seems now more certain than ever that the bloody experience of Vietnam is to end in a stalemate," he told his millions of viewers after the surprise attacks known as the Tet Offensive rocked South Vietnam, and following his own reporting trip there.)

My parents subscribed to both dailies, each owned by a prosperous Buffalo family. One carried Ann Landers's advice column; the other published her sister, known as Dear Abby. One supported Richard Nixon until nearly the end of his ill-fated and corrupt presidency. The other wanted him gone much sooner. The news all seemed personal, close to home. In these pre-internet days, it didn't come to us immediately via iPhones in our pockets, but it reached us, and touched us, nonetheless.

When I was in first grade, I was sitting at my desk at Our Lady of Victory Elementary School when our teacher, Sister Romana, a diminutive nun of the Sisters of St. Joseph order, was called out of our classroom. She returned to tell us that President Kennedy had been shot to death in Texas and she was sending us home for the day. Our school sat next to the parish's grand European-style basilica, which dominated the Lackawanna skyline; here, the assassination of the first Roman Catholic president hit especially hard. My family members, like most of our Lackawanna neighbors, were observant Catholics; my father, a defense attorney, walked the short block to Mass at the basilica and received Communion every morning before heading to his firm's office in downtown Buffalo. Like my parents, most people in our blue-collar community were Democrats, with plenty of them members of the steelworkers union, though both of my mother's brothers, a doctor and a lawyer, were Republicans. At home, we talked and argued about all that was happening, with my father as the acknowledged expert on most subjects—everything from the seemingly endless Vietnam War to classic literature—but with opinions flowing freely from all five of us. I was the youngest, and always felt that I had less to contribute, but I was absorbing it all. I was reading the daily newspapers, too, or at least taking in the headlines.

Then came the Watergate scandal. Like most Americans and many Lackawanna residents, my family was glued to our one television set, a focal point of the living room, as we watched the Senate Watergate hearings, broadcast initially on every network, live and during the daytime hours. Later, the networks rotated coverage and public television replayed the hearings in the evening. You could hardly miss what was happening: 85 percent of households in the United States watched some part of the hearings. This high political drama played out for months as charges of corruption, even criminality, were leveled at Richard Nixon's administration, kicked off by a break-in at Democratic National Committee headquarters at the Watergate Complex in Washington, D.C. As the investigation unfolded, the players—Washington politicians—became as compelling and familiar to us as the characters of *The Sopranos,* or later still, *Mare of Easttown,* would be to generations several decades on. There was the folksy Sam Ervin, the conservative Democrat from North Carolina and chairman of the Senate Watergate Committee. There was the senator from Tennessee, Howard Baker, who, although a staunch Republican, put aside partisanship and embraced patriotism when he memorably asked, "What did the president know and when did he know it?" There was former White House counsel John Dean, the young preppie in his tortoiseshell glasses, who ultimately, and devastatingly, would characterize the scandal and its lie-filled cover-up as "a cancer on the presidency."

When the House of Representatives Judiciary Committee held its hearings, we were riveted by Barbara Jordan's soaring opening remarks about the Constitution, about being a Black woman in America, and about her obligation to her fellow citizens. It was a real-time lesson in civil rights, racial injustice, and governmental checks and balances. Her authoritative voice commanded attention as she talked movingly about her racial identity, and her mere presence as a Black woman was a stark contrast to the hearings' parade of white men. "I felt somehow for many years that George Washington and Alexander Hamilton just left me out by mistake," Jordan said. "But through the process of amendment, interpretation and court decision I have finally been included in 'We, the people.'" We could hear her conviction when she added: "My faith in the Constitution is whole, it is complete, it is total, and I am not going to sit here and be an idle spectator to the diminution, the subversion, the destruction of the Constitution." In 1974, a Black woman member of Congress was unusual enough, but Jordan was even more noteworthy because of this Judiciary Committee role that catapulted her onto the national stage. A lawyer in her late thirties, she was a first-term congresswoman who had grown up in segregated Texas and become the first woman and the first African American elected to Congress from her state.

My mother, in particular, seemed captivated by her eloquent passion. This admiration affected me. Barbara Jordan was my homemaker mother's idea of a powerful and accomplished woman of integrity, someone worthy of emulating. At a subconscious level, I took note. I had heard confusingly mixed messages as I was growing up about what a woman should be and do: Get married as soon as possible and have children? Have a successful career, but quit it, as my mother had done when she married? Do some kind of work in the public interest? But now, through the Watergate scandal, of all things, I absorbed an unspoken, but also unmuddied, message: Be like Barbara Jordan. Be brave, be authentic, make a difference, and have the courage of your convictions.

I was far from alone in my youthful reaction to the hearings. Timothy O'Brien, who would become an investigative business reporter for *The New York Times*, was twelve years old, attending a science camp in Illinois, where a camp staffer encouraged the youngsters to watch the Senate hearings. The drama and the characters affected Tim, just as they did me. "I remember Sam Ervin saying [of Nixon], when he thought his mic was off, 'He's just a goddamn liar,'" O'Brien recalled many years later when I interviewed him for a piece in *Columbia Journalism Review.* "Those televised hearings gave me one of my first civics lessons about checks and balances and holding power accountable."

O'Brien and I, and countless other Watergate-era kids, were drawn into our careers—and not just in journalism—by this high-stakes spectacle on Capitol Hill. Sherrilyn Ifill, the prominent civil rights lawyer, recalled that seeing Barbara Jordan's Watergate appearance on TV changed her life, too: "A woman, a Black woman, with a voice of absolute moral authority . . . very, very powerful for me in thinking about who I could be as a woman." Ifill became the president of the NAACP Legal Defense and Educational Fund, founded by Thurgood Marshall, the first Black justice of the U.S. Supreme Court. In 2021, she told *Your Hometown* podcaster Kevin Burke that Barbara Jordan's televised prominence was part of "how gender roles . . . began to open up, particularly in the early seventies."

As a teenager, I was living through a period of huge societal change brought about by the civil rights movement, second-wave feminism, and the counterculture revolution. Journalism may not have been as high-profile as civil rights activism as a way to create reform, but as Watergate made abundantly clear, it certainly could be an effective way of holding power accountable.

After all, the dogged investigative reporting of two *Washington Post* staffers, Bob Woodward and Carl Bernstein, lit the kindling that led to Nixon's eventual resignation, as they revealed the White House cover-up of the break-in and all kinds of other government malfeasance. Granted, my juvenile understanding of this was somewhat murky; it wasn't until the movie version of *All the President's Men* came out in 1976 that it all came into sharper focus. Journalism began to look downright fascinating as Robert Redford and Dustin Hoffman, in the lead roles as the reporters, dashed from office to underground parking garage, or worked their sources on deadline in the newsroom. The ringing phones and clattering typewriters added to the ambiance of a movie set that uncannily resembled the real-life *Post* newsroom of that era. Journalism seemed not only crucial for the good of the nation's democracy but also enticingly glamorous. There were untold numbers of us, the budding journalists of the Watergate generation; we flooded into newsrooms large and small after seeing the movie and connecting it to the real-life history we had witnessed only a few years before.

How could we resist the intrigue? "I wanted to be Robert Redford moving that ceramic pot," O'Brien recalled, referring to Woodward's secret signal to his confidential source, jocularly known in the *Post* newsroom as "Deep Throat." (That moniker was a play on the reporting term "deep background"—an agreement between reporter and source that is not quite as restrictive as "off the record"—but also a bawdy reference to a then-current pornographic movie.) O'Brien remembers thinking, "Wow, these are the guys that set everything in motion." I knew exactly what he meant: These two young reporters not only revealed corruption at the highest level of government and played a part in bringing down a corrupt president but also kicked off an intense new era of investigative journalism. And, despite the mostly male newsroom staff on display in the film, it never occurred to me that being a woman would be an impediment to joining this ultra-cool club. Maybe that was another Watergate-era message from seeing Barbara Jordan's strength and authenticity: *Seize your power.* It's certainly notable that a twenty-six-year-old Hillary Rodham also had a Watergate role, though I wasn't aware of it at the time. Not long out of Yale Law School, she worked on the impeachment inquiry staff of the House Judiciary Committee. Sitting in a windowless hotel room across the street from Congress, Hillary was one of the first to hear the Oval Office tapes that would bring Nixon down. Yes, Watergate's tentacles reached far and wide.

During the summer of the Senate hearings, my eldest brother, David, home from college, asked me what I thought I might like to do as a career. We were sitting in his bedroom, which, like my brother Phil's, featured curtains with a ships-and-maps pattern that evoked Magellan's circumnavigation of the globe. (Another unspoken gender message, that boys should be adventurous and set off to see the world? My room, by contrast, featured girly pink gingham, and—what's galling to me now—it lacked a desk like the big sturdy ones both of my brothers had. In adulthood, I've always made sure I had a substantial desk.) I told David what interested me, and what I thought I might be good at. Reading. Words. Knowing what's going on. Communicating. In one of my life's more significant moments, my brother looked me in the eye and offered a single word of advice, as if it were perfectly obvious and preordained: "Journalism." I wasn't quite sure how to move forward on the suggestion, or even fully sure what it meant.

Luckily, my all-girls high school, Buffalo's Nardin Academy, had a student newspaper and an inspiring advisor, Joanne Langan. She was married to the school's headmaster, Michael Langan, who shared my Lackawanna roots and became a mentor, too. Mrs. Langan was an enlightened English teacher who, long before most schools had diversified their reading lists beyond the canon of dead white men, had us reading Anne Moody's *Coming of Age in Mississippi,* Joyce Carol Oates's *them,* and the poems of Maya Angelou. Apparently, she saw something promising in me, and pushed me to put my name forward to edit the student newspaper, *Kaleidoscope.* The year after Nixon resigned the presidency in disgrace (escaping inevitable impeachment and likely conviction), Nardin's faculty and newspaper staff named me the editor in chief. Classroom 210 became my first newsroom—the first of many—and one of my best friends, Sheila Rooney, was my second-in-command. (We also shared the captaincy of Nardin's varsity basketball team.) As editor, in addition to making story assignments and ferrying the pasted-up newspaper pages to an off-campus printing plant, I wrote editorials on serious subjects. One reluctantly supported President Gerald Ford's decision to pardon Nixon, thus sparing the country endless turmoil and division. Another considered the merits of the court-ordered busing to integrate Buffalo's schools; this was a controversial topic locally and in many parts of the country.

All the while, I was looking ahead. I had asked my uncle,

the managing editor of *The Cleveland Press*, the evening paper at the other end of Lake Erie, how to get started for real as a working journalist. I was lucky to have a close family member showing me what a career in journalism could look like; even better, it was obvious that Bob Sullivan enjoyed his job, which contrasted with my father's observation that his own profession, the law, too often was nothing but "drudgery." My uncle insisted that the best foundation for journalism was a liberal arts education, not an undergraduate journalism degree; I could follow that with a master's degree in journalism like the one he had earned at Columbia University. I took his advice to heart.

The gender issues at play in the late 1970s for an ambitious girl like me were complicated, though I never stopped to think about them too hard since I was busy listening to music, playing sports, and hanging out with my friends. Maybe I didn't have the internal language to grapple with the role of women in American life. I knew this much: My mother had given up a promising future as a women's fashion buyer for a department store to get married and start a family in the 1950s; she was a rising star, scheduled for her first buying trip to Paris and Milan, when she resigned at age thirty to marry my father. Growing up, I was aware that she had some regrets about abandoning her career; but, as an American whose parents were born in Lebanon (soon after immigrating, her father opened a men's clothing store in Lackawanna, which became the family's livelihood), she channeled her urges for upward mobility into her children's lives. She propelled my older brothers toward academic achievement and careers in respected professions. Taking heed, they became a doctor and a lawyer. But she thought I might be best suited to become, as she put it, an "executive secretary." What she *really* wanted, it seemed clear, was for me to marry well (someone like my brothers would do fine) and to have children. This double standard, however, had a hidden advantage: Since she was pressing no specific vocation on me, I was forced—and also free—to imagine my own path. My brothers went to prestigious colleges in Massachusetts; I was initially restricted to someplace closer to home. I spent freshman year at Le Moyne College in Syracuse, a Jesuit school with a fine reputation, but one that I was determined to outgrow. I yearned for a major city and a big-name school. After earning close to perfect grades at Le Moyne, I persuaded my parents to let me transfer as a sophomore to Georgetown University; it would appeal to them, I calculated, in that it was also run by Jesuits, the scholarly order of Roman Catholic priests to which my family had close ties.

My plan worked. Suddenly, still a teenager, I was living in a Georgetown University dormitory only a few miles from the sites of those dramatic Capitol Hill scenes that had mesmerized me just a few years earlier during the Watergate hearings. And the big-journalism world of Washington was right there for the taking. Soon I was riding the city bus from campus to a part-time clerk's job downtown at Gannett News Service. Like a smaller version of the Associated Press, the service provided news to the chain's newspapers around the country. I did whatever tasks were sent my way, mostly typing articles from the bureau's Washington correspondents into the computer system for national distribution. Back at school, I was a reporter covering the medical-school beat for

The Hoya, the more traditional of Georgetown's two student newspapers; later, I became the arts editor of *The Georgetown Voice*, an alternative student newspaper that styled itself after *The Village Voice*, where I assigned theater and music reviews to student critics.

After my junior year, the Gannett connection paid off. My mentor in the Washington bureau, a generous editor named Anita Sama, helped me get a summer internship at the *Niagara Gazette* in Niagara Falls, New York, one of the papers in Gannett's national chain. I might have spent the summer writing concert reviews and feature stories from the compact newsroom, almost within view of the cascading waters of the natural wonder. That's how my *Gazette* internship started out. I was having fun, answering to the encouraging young editor for features, Susan LoTempio, and finding it hard to believe I was collecting a paycheck. Getting bylines and hanging around with the *Gazette*'s wisecracking wordsmiths suited me well.

But then disaster struck, quite literally. In mid-summer, President Jimmy Carter declared the city of Niagara Falls a national disaster area. An environmental calamity was unfolding in the Love Canal neighborhood, where for decades local chemical companies had dumped huge quantities of toxic waste. The long-buried poisons had begun bubbling up in residents' basements and yards. Children and adults were getting sick, as *Gazette* reporter Michael Brown had been reporting for years without garnering much attention. Once the chemical leaks and the residents' illnesses became too obvious to ignore, Love Canal became a huge national news story, and maybe the biggest story ever for the *Gazette*. The paper's small staff was so overwhelmed that the paper's city editor, Dave Pollack, had little choice but to assign me, an inexperienced intern, to cover some aspects of it. He must have been desperate; I didn't have much confidence, but I stumbled through whatever assignments came my way.

A journalism axiom dictates that there's "no crying in newsrooms," but I shed tears that summer. The formidable reporting duo of David Shribman and Paul MacClennan from our big-city competition, *The Buffalo Evening News,* had scooped us *again* on yet another important part of the fast-developing Love Canal story. (Shribman, then only in his mid-twenties, was a big talent, and eventually a Pulitzer Prize winner.) I was a competitive person, whether on the basketball court or in the newsroom, so it hurt to have our head handed to us, day after day, at the *Gazette.* Apparently, my tears of frustration didn't alienate my bosses or make them think less of me. At the end of the summer, the *Gazette*'s top editor, Fletcher Clarke, someone I had barely spoken to all summer, called me into his office. He startled me by offering a full-time reporting job—to begin immediately. Since that would have meant dropping out of college, I decided against it, an easy enough call, and went back to Washington for senior year.

After that summer, I knew that I was in the right field. The *Gazette*'s job offer and my front-page stories had boosted my confidence. I had an affirming sense, too, that journalists were held in high regard. Not by everyone, of course. Nixon had kept an enemies list that included media people, and his vice president, Spiro Agnew, famously had ranted about journalists as "nattering nabobs of negativism." Roger Ailes, who would help found Fox News two decades later, had given Nixon and his cronies advice on how to depict journalists as out-of-touch liberals, not quite "the enemy of the people" yet, but getting there. The nativist populism that would help elect Donald Trump was festering. With its growing resentment of the press and other supposedly elite institutions, it bubbled under the surface of American society like the toxins at Love Canal. Still, that mindset wasn't yet pervasive.

Gallup, the public opinion polling company, began measuring trust in the national press in the 1970s. The trust number, already high, ticked upward in the years after Watergate and the publication of the Pentagon Papers, the secret history of the United States' disastrous involvement in Vietnam, first by *The New York Times* and then by *The Washington Post*. The national newspapers were ably performing their watchdog role, the TV networks were following suit, and the vast majority of citizens seemed to appreciate it. In 1976, two years after Nixon's forced resignation, an impressive 72 percent of Americans had a great deal or a fair amount of trust in the press—and the numbers would never again reach that height. Of course, this was also an era in which other institutions were held in relatively high regard, too: schools, churches, business, law enforcement, even government to some extent.

Journalism certainly wasn't despised; far from it. When I told friends and family members that I was planning to be a reporter, that I'd been the top editor of my high school paper, and that I had gotten paid to write stories about the Love Canal disaster, they seemed impressed. After being wait-listed at Columbia's graduate school of journalism (a crushing blow, since I had assumed for years that I would get my master's degree there), I accepted a scholarship at Northwestern University's highly regarded Medill School. Was journalism school a necessity? Definitely not, but I've always been glad I had a master's degree, had formal education in media law and ethics, and had the chance to spend time in the Chicago area. During one semester, I got to do some reporting from Washington, D.C., for two small newspapers as part of the Medill News Service, in which students worked as national correspondents and had their work published on a near-daily basis. After an internship at one of my hometown dailies, *The Buffalo Evening News,* turned into a full-time reporting job, I covered hard-news beats—business, county government, public education—and broke my share of stories, including an investigation of financial malfeasance in Erie County government.

By the end of the 1980s, I had been named an assistant city editor, supervising a six-man (yes, all-male) team of politics and government reporters. That was stressful at times; the veteran politics reporter, in particular, didn't much like taking guidance from an editor barely in her thirties with much less experience than he had. We worked it out, though, and supervising this group meant that I had started my climb up the newsroom management ladder.

Not only was I mostly having fun, reveling in the newsroom atmosphere, but I also felt the reporting and editing work was important for my city and region. We were keeping powerful institutions honest, or at least helping to do so. I got no sense that I had entered a field that most people mistrusted. As the 1990s approached, many local newspapers were financially successful; profit margins well above 30 percent were nothing unusual. And the press was undeniably important in the United States, perhaps not beloved but recognized as vital to the way American democracy functioned. What's more, journalism offered a viable career path: not a great way to get rich but certainly a way to earn a living wage. As a bonus, it struck me as exceedingly cool.

2

Little Miss Lifestyles Breaks Out

It's 1995, and I am sitting in an auditorium at the offices of *The Buffalo News,* watching in horror as my boss takes credit for my idea. To make matters worse (or possibly comical), it's an idea he hates. He is Murray Light, the top editor of the paper. And at this moment I am the assistant managing editor for features, which is a typical job for an ambitious woman in newspaper journalism in the mid-1990s. The features department, sometimes known as "lifestyles," is where arts criticism and some of the most creative writing reside, and it's often a place for experimentation, since the *serious* people in the newsroom are all preoccupied with City Hall corruption and national politics, and therefore not paying attention. But, as a place for this "softer" journalism, the features department doesn't get nearly as much respect as the centers of hard news: the city or metro desk, the Washington bureau, the statehouse bureau in Albany, or, at larger papers, the foreign bureaus in Paris, London, or Beijing.

I enjoyed my job and loved my thirty-person staff of talented critics and features writers. But, after a few years, I found myself itching for a wider role at the paper. I had told Murray that I wanted to be put on the publisher's small committee assigned to think outside the box, as the management cliché went, about "reinventing" the paper. Circulation was falling, and something needed to be done to stem the losses. Murray agreed readily enough. So I immersed myself in research about readership trends and brainstormed with colleagues. Soon, along with my friends in the graphic design department, I cooked up a radically redesigned front page. There were no stories on it, just teasers to what was inside the paper. It was flashy and engaging, and it looked nothing like the stodgy, traditional *Buffalo Evening News* where I had come to work fifteen years earlier as a summer intern, and where many of the news stories I'd written as a hard-news reporter, covering business, education, and government beats, had appeared on the front page. The top editors of the paper were appalled by my redesigned atrocity, as they saw it. But they had a problem. The paper's publisher, Stan Lipsey, who outranked them, had heard something about this buzzy thing, asked to see it, and, heaven forbid, he loved it. So did his wife, Judith, who was the paper's marketing guru, though she was not on staff. Stan demanded that Murray and his top deputies present it to the newsroom and move toward rolling it out to the public—which is why my boss was standing on a stage taking credit for my idea, which he hated. Privately, Murray had chastised me: The redesign was a "concept car," he fumed, a crazy idea never meant to leave the auto dealer's showroom. Nevertheless, at this moment—in front of about

150 journalists who worked for him, and under duress from *his* boss—he was trying hard to sound as if he believed in it and had come up with it himself.

At one point during his presentation, a sports columnist not especially noted for his respect for corporate authority piped up: "I understand Margaret Sullivan had something to do with this project. I'd like to hear her vision." I was more than willing, and halfway out of my seat, thinking of how to sell the merits of this approach, when Murray shut it down in seven words: "Margaret has nothing to do with this." I sank back down. As I wrote in my journal: "A punch in the gut would have felt considerably less jarring." He tried to soften his brusqueness with a vague remark about my possible involvement in the future. That didn't help, since he had already uttered the all-too-memorable sound bite. He did, however, ask me to describe for the assembled staff a new section for kids that was being planned—a safe and appropriate use of my skills, from his viewpoint. I ranted in my journal about "the Little Miss Lifestyles Syndrome—the warm and soothing feeling that no doubt comes from seeing me firmly in my place as the talented and docile editor of the former women's section."

The Buffalo News never did roll that concept-car redesign out of the showroom. More traditional ideas prevailed, and maybe that was for the best. But a couple of years later, I finally reaped the benefits of that venture: After a fierce competition, I was named the paper's first woman managing editor, the number two job in the newsroom, and therefore the clear heir apparent to Murray as chief editor, who was due to retire the following year. What had hurt in the moment served me well in the long run, because I acquired a reputation for thinking creatively and taking risks.

Murray had been good to me most of the time I worked for him. He and his managing editor, Foster Spencer, had hired me straight out of school, which was unusual at the time. Over the years, Murray tolerated rookie mistakes I made as a reporter, gave me several promotions, and encouraged me to work a flexible schedule when my children were infants and toddlers. He was a person of integrity and a capable top editor who clearly recognized that I had something to offer. But when Murray announced he was going to retire in a year or so, it was clear that he wanted one of his longtime deputies, Ed Cuddihy, to be his successor. A no-nonsense former city editor, and a fine newsman who had spent his entire career at the paper, Ed would have built on everything Murray had done without turning anything on its head. He also had the advantage of being a middle-aged man with decades of experience, whereas I was significantly younger and a woman. The paper had never had a woman editor or managing editor. I had to figure out how to maneuver around that, since Murray would have a role in naming the next editor. Luckily for me, he wouldn't be the one to make the final choice. That was Stan Lipsey, the publisher, along with the *News*'s president, Warren Colville. I wanted the top job badly. Looking back, I don't think my reasons were particularly lofty. I was motivated by a desire for growth and advancement; I wanted to have a wider influence at the paper and in the city; and I thought that I would be the best choice for the paper's staff and for the readership.

I knew, though, that this promotion could cause problems at home. My then-husband was the editor of the paper's Sunday magazine; we had met in the newsroom when we were both reporters. He was less than enthusiastic about my quest to become the paper's editor. Mostly he opposed the idea, in part because our children were young and by its nature the job would be consuming. Even before I became top editor, it wasn't uncommon for us both to be awakened at night by a phone call from the on-duty editor to tell me about some major breaking story and to consult about where it should be displayed or what the headline should say. I had felt for years the difficulties of balancing motherhood with my job; I was always dashing from the pediatrician's office or the school Halloween parade to an editorial board meeting or the latest staff disruption, often feeling that I wasn't giving enough to either role.

Still, this was the opportunity of a lifetime, one that I felt called to pursue. So I campaigned for the job, making the case to the decision-makers that I would bring a fresh approach that would benefit the paper and serve its readers. I wrote memos, some serious, some lighthearted—even a meant-to-amuse "Ten Reasons Why I Should Be the Next Editor"—and relentlessly talked about my vision for the paper. I wanted to make the journalism more enterprising and public-spirited, and the presentation more appealing; I wanted more direct engagement with our readership. I wanted to establish the paper's first investigative team and do more watchdog journalism. *The Buffalo News* was a well-respected paper, but it also was a little dull, with a lot of attention to established institutions in the region. Our longtime rival, the *Courier-Express*, was livelier and more informal in its tone and presentation. But after 1982, it was out of business. I thought it was high time for the *News* to be edgier, to have a more conversational tone when appropriate, and to pay much more attention to the diverse communities we served.

Apparently, I persuaded them. When my appointment as editor was announced in 1999, much was made of my becoming one of the few women to run a regional newsroom; at just over forty, I was one of the youngest, too. At the one hundred largest newspapers in the United States, only thirteen chief editors were women. In Buffalo, this was a history-making first, and local women's groups took note. My office filled up with congratulatory floral arrangements; one, from a group of women lawyers, came with a small card that read, "We hear the sound of shattering glass."

At a *Buffalo News* picnic shortly after my appointment was announced, I stood on a stage, addressing the company's employees, not just journalists but advertising, production, and circulation staffers, too. A newsroom photographer captured an image that I cherish: My six-year-old daughter, Grace, stands at my side, looking adorably cute and right at home, leaning forward to peer at the audience while I speak into a standing microphone. For that moment, at least, all the elements of life seemed to be in harmony.

My twenty-year marriage came to an end in 2007, something that was painful for all of us. These days, many years later, I'm grateful that the family relationships have endured, and extremely proud to see my son and daughter thriving in their lives as they both pursue careers in public interest law. I've often asked myself if my ambition was a contributing factor in the marriage's demise. The answer, unavoidably, is yes, though our problems certainly were broader and deeper. And when I've stopped to wonder whether a man would have had a very different experience in similar circumstances, I get the same answer: an unequivocal yes.

I spent three decades at *The Buffalo News,* the last dozen as top editor. I certainly never intended to stay that long, but there was always another challenge: a new beat to cover, a great story to write, another step up the management ladder. And the final chapter—getting to lead my hometown paper as top editor—was one of the great privileges of my life. Every day, after parking in an outdoor lot within view of Lake Erie (sometimes covered with ice, sometimes sparkling in the summer sunshine), I would walk up the three flights of stairs to the newsroom. I liked to use the back door, the one closest to where the massive presses churned out hundreds of thousands of papers every day. I could smell the ink and hear the clanking of the freight elevator. As I emerged from the stairwell into the newsroom, I often thought of the J. D. Salinger character Buddy Glass, who came to regard *his* workplace, a small-college classroom, as a "piece of holy ground." I felt the same.

The top editor's position certainly had been a long time coming. When I graduated from Northwestern in 1980, I had internship offers at both of my hometown papers in Buffalo:

the *Courier-Express* and the *Evening News.* I asked my father which he thought I should take, and he replied without hesitation that the *Evening News* was "the dominant paper." I took the *News* internship and was hired at the end of the summer. My father had certainly called it right. In 1982, the *Courier* would announce that it was going out of business; once the investor (and eventual billionaire) Warren Buffett bought the evening paper, a fierce newspaper war—a battle for survival—was joined. In that era, there was enough ad revenue and reader interest for only one newspaper in most American cities. Second newspapers were going out of business all across the country. Buffett and his Buffalo representatives struck a death blow when they started a Sunday paper to siphon off some of the advertising revenue from the *Courier*'s most lucrative day of the week.

It turned out to be a tough year for the Buffalo area, since not only did its beloved morning paper go out of business, but Bethlehem Steel decided to shutter its huge steel mill in Lackawanna, the small city just south of Buffalo where I had grown up. Both events were devastating news for the region, and in both cases they were portents of what was ahead: the sharp decline of American manufacturing, along with the loss of blue-collar, union jobs that could support a family on one income; and the decades-long decline of local newspapers, a downward spiral that continues to this day. I felt both events deeply. My mother and father still lived in Lackawanna, so the steel-plant closing felt very personal. I had many friends at the *Courier,* one of the two papers I had grown up reading. The journalists there scattered all over the country, part of a Buffalo diaspora that went on for many years. I lost my chief competitor, Joan Verdon, who covered the education beat, and whose scoops I lived in fear of, as I hoped she did mine.

I lived in a second-floor apartment in Buffalo by then, and would race down the stairs every morning as soon as I woke to grab the morning paper and scan the front page for a Verdon byline. One of those above the fold on the front page made for a bad start to my day; it meant that I would be playing catch-up, and that the pressure would be intense to find some piece of education news that she didn't know about. By reporting it, I could then make *her* life miserable. And so it went.

I also wrote longer features, ones that had nothing to do with education. At one point I went to Washington to report a profile of Daniel Patrick Moynihan for our Sunday magazine. The Harvard professor turned New York senator spoke in eloquent riddles as I interviewed him; I scribbled furiously, and later realized I had next to nothing comprehensible to quote him on. At one point, I retreated to the bathroom in his Senate chambers and looked at my notebook in despair. My tape-recorded interviews with him didn't yield much more that was useful. I somehow wrote a cover story for the magazine, but it relied heavily on background reporting about the senator, whose intellectualism and originality of political thought made him both widely admired and polarizing. Decades later, as my train would arrive at the new Moynihan

Train Hall at New York's Penn Station, I'd conjure the erudite senator in his trademark bow tie and remember all the trouble I had interviewing him.

In 1998, Moynihan announced that he would be retiring from the Senate after twenty-four years, and he tapped Hillary Clinton—still the First Lady at that point—as his preferred successor. Not everybody agreed that this was a good idea. Plenty of New Yorkers, along with the Clintons' many political enemies in Washington, depicted her as an opportunistic carpetbagger. After all, she had grown up in Illinois and spent her professional life in Arkansas and Washington, D.C. The Clintons had only recently bought a house in Westchester County's Chappaqua, north of New York City. To try to counter this criticism, which could have been a political death sentence, she started what she called a listening tour across New York State. The tour brought her, among other places, to our editorial board meetings in Buffalo, a few months after I had been named editor. When she entered the third-floor conference room, where we held the daily meetings to plan the next day's front page, I cringed when Stan Lipsey, the publisher and my direct boss, greeted her with a kiss on the cheek. That was too cozy a relationship between newspaper publisher and politician for my taste, but Stan always did things his own way. (He once passed around a photocopied list of "dumb blonde" jokes at the weekly lunch meeting, where there were only two women, including me, at a table of a dozen newspaper executives; I complained afterward, and it didn't happen again.)

I hadn't met Hillary before, but I wondered with some trepidation if she was aware that only a few months earlier I had made national news by asking then-President Bill Clinton a most unwelcome question at the annual conference of the American Society of Newspaper Editors in Washington. President Clinton, who had been impeached in 1998 and acquitted the following year, had been trying to change the subject as he spoke to hundreds of news editors. I conferred with our Washington bureau chief, Douglas Turner, and we came up with a provocative question for me to pose: If his vice president, Al Gore, was elected later that year, would Clinton ask for a pardon for any possible crimes committed during his presidency?

I raced up to one of several standing microphones in a huge hotel ballroom so I could ask one of the first questions, identified myself as the editor of *The Buffalo News,* and fired away. The president reacted angrily, smacking the lectern in apparent frustration; this was clearly something he didn't want to address, since it put the attention of the nation's newspaper editors—and thus the nation—squarely back on his impeachment for perjury and obstruction of justice; that sordid saga had begun with his affair with a White House intern, Monica Lewinsky. But he had no choice under the circumstances, and he answered the question: No, he wouldn't ask for, or accept, a pardon.

This was news. Not only did the story about his answer appear on the front pages of *The New York Times, USA Today,* and *The Washington Post* the next day, but some of this national coverage identified me as the questioner—as if it were truly remarkable for a feisty woman editor from the provinces to challenge the president of the United States. My journal entry from April 14, 2000, jotted down at Reagan National

Airport as I left Washington, began: "Well, it looks like I've used up a few of my fifteen minutes of fame." I noted that I hadn't slept much: "I kept seeing myself at the microphone. Rehearsing after the fact."

If Hillary had any recollection of my encounter with her husband—I think she must have—she didn't give a hint in that *Buffalo News* editorial board meeting. She was cordial and businesslike. After it concluded, she asked me quietly if I could point her to the ladies' room; we were, after all, almost the only women in the room. Rather than just point, I accompanied her across the newsroom. We chatted as we went, a walk-and-talk scene out of *The West Wing,* and I could feel the newsroom staff's eyes on us. (She would go on to win the Senate seat in 2000, and again in 2006, but wouldn't finish her second term because, soon after the 2008 election, President Obama named her secretary of state.) Hillary, always well prepared and knowledgeable, made a point of observing to me that there weren't many top newspaper editors in the nation who were women. I appreciated that she knew such a thing, and her observation accomplished what perhaps it was intended to do: give me a sense that we had something in common as groundbreakers.

Often portrayed as cold or unlikeable, she came off to me as quite the opposite. She was personable and easy to identify with, as well as in complete command of Western New York minutiae. She could talk in detail about the region's bridges and water treatment facilities, and about its economic troubles stemming from the loss of manufacturing jobs like the ones, years before, at Bethlehem Steel in Lackawanna. But she also was willing to speak personally, and even in that short chat as we walked to the ladies' room, we mentioned our children; mine were in grade school at the time, while her daughter, Chelsea, was at Stanford University. It went unexpressed, but seemed understood, that we both had had the experience of being the first woman to do a particular job or be the only woman in a roomful of decision-makers.

The morning of September 11, 2001, was a sunny, almost cloudless day in Buffalo, just as it was across the state in lower Manhattan. It started off as a slow news day. In our regular morning news meeting, we editors scraped around for how to put together the front page of the afternoon editions. But when the second plane hit the World Trade Center, I stood in the middle of the newsroom and mentally flipped through the file cards of past news events, looking for a way to measure this. The Columbine school massacre in 1999? The Oklahoma City bombing in 1995? There was nothing to compare. I hadn't been alive when Pearl Harbor was attacked, but that was the only comparison I could come up with. The editors jumped into action, tearing up the front page of the afternoon editions, and immediately began planning special coverage. This was, of course, a huge national and international story, but for us, as New Yorkers, also a local one. Crews of Buffalo-area firefighters and emergency workers were headed downstate to help—and there were local people missing and presumed dead. I soon found out that among them was Sean Rooney. He was the brother of my close friend Sheila Rooney, who had worked on the Nardin *Kaleidoscope* with me. We quickly sent journalists to the scene in downtown

Manhattan. Chaos reigned. Life, and journalism, were never the same. At home, we talked to the children about what had happened. Alex, still in grade school but always an old soul, had a characteristic answer when we asked if he was scared: "I don't feel immediately threatened."

Not long afterward, my childhood hometown dominated the national headlines, as the Justice Department identified what it called a "sleeper cell" of potential terrorists only a mile from where I grew up. The Lackawanna Six were a half-dozen men of Yemeni descent who had traveled to Afghanistan for training, some of them reportedly even meeting with Osama bin Laden, and then returned to the United States. Under the Patriot Act, which was railroaded into existence mere weeks after 9/11, all sorts of previously forbidden snooping on American citizens was suddenly allowed, and this helped to ensnare these locally born and raised men. They all pleaded guilty and went to prison, and the Bush administration touted this as a legal and intelligence triumph that may have avoided another terrorist attack.

Perhaps it did, but the Patriot Act was government overreach with a serious downside, like the perfectly legal but morally suspect warrantless wiretapping of American citizens that would eventually make big news. But in the wake of 9/11, everyone—including the press—was expected to get on board the patriotism express without asking too many questions. For the most part, journalists did just that, to their eventual shame. At *The Buffalo News,* the arrests, prosecution, and sentencing of the Lackawanna Six were a huge continuing story that dominated our front pages for weeks and months. And for me, it was literally close to home—the very place where my childhood friends and I had watched the sky turn orange each evening as they dumped the slag at Bethlehem Steel.

In the years that followed, during my time as editor, our newsroom did crucial work, even as the newspaper business started to experience financial troubles, both locally and nationally, because of the loss of print advertising revenue. I had established the paper's first investigative team, and we embarked on many projects, including one called "The High Cost of Being Poor." Buffalo was one of the poorest cities in the nation, and its children suffered the worst; two of every five children in the city lived below the poverty line, and the public schools were, in the words of another series we did, "Halls of Inequity." Rich kids could get a good education in Buffalo; poor kids struggled for meager resources. Maybe we couldn't fix that problem, but at least we could show people how bad it was.

The Buffalo area's strong disagreements over abortion rights dominated these years as well. In this heavily Roman Catholic city and region, contentious protests outside local abortion clinics were a common sight; in 1992, Mayor Jimmy Griffin, a conservative Democrat, invited the anti-abortion activists Operation Rescue to put on a major event. Thousands of out-of-town protesters, representing both sides of the controversy, showed up for an event called the Spring of Life, attracting national attention and resulting in nearly two hundred arrests as anti-abortion protesters tried to block access to clinics. Then, in 1998, a local physician and abortion provider, Barnett Slepian, was assassinated in his own home by a sniper. Slepian was making soup in his kitchen after returning from a memorial service for his father when he was shot through a window; he died almost immediately. It was a huge national story, one whose developments and repercussions we would cover for years, including when the killer, James Kopp, gave a jailhouse confession to two of our reporters, claiming he had only wanted to wound Slepian to keep him from performing more abortions. Kopp was found guilty of murder by a Buffalo-area judge; his sentence was twenty-five years to life in prison. Everything about this coverage was fraught with high emotion and subject to extreme criticism, including within the newsroom itself, where conservative Catholics sat side by side with progressive feminists.

Among the biggest stories was the 2009 crash of a commercial airliner in which fifty people died; our Washington and Albany reporters, Jerry Zremski and Tom Precious, were indefatigable in digging out the causes. Their reporting on the role of pilot fatigue and training helped bring about national reforms that were credited with making flying safer for everyone. As they learned of the causes, the families of the Colgan Air Flight 3407 victims relentlessly pushed Congress to pass sweeping legislation designed to prevent future disasters, including the creation of a pilot-record database and the requirement that flight crews get adequate rest time between flights. Those reforms were tremendously effective. In the two decades before the Buffalo disaster, U.S. airlines had experienced a major crash, on average, every seventeen months. By contrast, in the decade after reform (the 2010 passage of an aviation safety law), they haven't suffered a single such accident. In terms of human lives, the difference is dramatic: 1,186 people died in those commercial plane crashes in the earlier two decades. The following decade saw only one such death and it was caused by a jet window that shattered.

This was the essence of local journalism with lifesaving impact: a Buffalo-area catastrophe, deep sorrow over hometown victims, and crucial national reforms rooted in the dogged journalism that followed over many months. Our journalism had helped make flying safer for everyone. Again, I couldn't help but take it personally. In a sickening twist of fate, one of the Flight 3407 victims was Beverly Eckert, the widow of Sean Rooney, who had died in the World Trade Center attack and who was the brother of my high school friend, Sheila Rooney. More bizarre still, Beverly was flying to Buffalo to award a scholarship in her late husband's name at his alma mater, Canisius High School—the same school from which my father, my brothers, and my son had graduated. At least I knew that we at *The Buffalo News* had done everything in our power to prevent something similar from happening again.

For many consecutive years while I was in charge, the New York News Publishers Association recognized the *News* with its top award for distinguished public service journalism; we competed in the same large-circulation category as the big papers in New York City and on Long Island. It made me incredibly proud of the staff to win that recognition year after year; journalism in the public interest, after all, is our highest calling. This recognition meant that, at least some of the time, we were fulfilling our mission. After the brilliant political cartoonist Tom Toles left *The Buffalo News* for *The Washington Post*, I hired Adam Zyglis, a twenty-two-year-old illustrator and summer intern, who in time would win our paper a Pulitzer Prize.

Amid the triumphs and satisfactions, of course, we made mistakes. Sometimes they were largely my fault, as with one aspect of our coverage of a mass shooting in downtown Buffalo in 2010. Eight people had been shot, four of them killed, outside City Grill, a restaurant where a wedding anniversary was being celebrated. A fifth man would die years later after being paralyzed as a result of his injuries. All the victims were Black. For days after the shooting, no one knew who the shooter was or what the motive was. As alarmed city residents tried to piece together what had happened, the paper published and prominently displayed a story detailing the criminal backgrounds of some of the victims, on the grounds that this information could be a part of the puzzle. The Black community was furious, accusing the *News* of deepening the pain of family and friends who were mourning and burying their loved ones. They were right. The story unintentionally put the blame in precisely the wrong place. I tried to make amends by arranging with a Black minister, Rev. Darius Pridgen, to come out to his church, True Bethel Baptist, to speak with some of his congregation.

It was not the small gathering I had sought; instead, seven hundred community members, some carrying accusatory signs, were there to confront me, not only about this story but also about the way the paper had covered their neighborhoods and communities for decades, long before I was editor. Our story and the placement of it had been harsh and insensitive. I learned a lot that evening from Buffalo residents like Cheryl Stevens, whose son-in-law was among the dead. "I feel that we were victimized twice," she told me in that public forum. "What you did to us was you poured salt on the wounds that had not even healed."

If anything provided a measure of solace on that difficult evening, it was the racial diversity of our newsroom staff, something that I had set out to improve through aggressive hiring and promotion. Many of the journalists of color in the newsroom decided of their own accord to come to the meeting, in part to show moral support for me since they knew I would be under fire. I was deeply touched by their presence; I can hardly imagine how much more difficult that evening would have been without it. Rev. Pridgen later told me that this made a difference to him, too: "I quickly scanned the staff, and when I saw diversity, it started to change the narrative in my mind." All of these events together turned into what he called "a healing moment." Chastened, I went back to the paper to put some reforms in place: training for our journalists on reporting more equitably and sensitively; covering the city's East Side in more thorough and considerate ways; forming a citizens council to bring complaints and ideas to the forefront.

Painful as the whole chapter was, it helped me understand the turmoil in newsrooms and around the country a decade later when George Floyd was murdered in Minneapolis and protests erupted everywhere. Far too often, as we had done in

Buffalo, the news coverage had the effect of blaming the victims. Black men who had died at the hands of police were described in news stories as "no angel," with their criminal records or personal flaws emphasized. I had learned the lesson once and for all, and was able to write about it with more empathy and insight when the issues came up again and again, particularly in the deaths of Trayvon Martin in Sanford, Florida, or Michael Brown in Ferguson, Missouri, as well as George Floyd's. "By seeking and blundering, we learn," wrote Goethe. Luckily for me, I got a chance not only to learn but also to move forward with what I knew. I'm not sure an editor today could have a similar opportunity for growth amid the heated rhetoric of Twitter.

The following year, I got an unexpected phone call from Ann Marie Lipinski, the former top editor of the *Chicago Tribune*. We had met briefly, and I admired her immensely, but we didn't know each other well. As the incoming co-chairwoman of the Pulitzer Prize board, she was calling to tell me that she and her board colleagues were inviting me to join them on that rarefied committee. This is the group that each year makes the final decisions on journalism's highest honors and on the coveted awards for fiction, nonfiction, poetry, drama, and music. I was thrilled, and a little disbelieving, at the invitation. Soon after, a veteran *News* copy editor, someone with plenty of strong opinions about journalism, surprised me when we crossed paths in the newsroom by proclaiming my Pulitzer appointment "overdue" and by offering some pointed advice: "Go knock some heads together."

Three decades earlier, as a college senior, I had cried bitter tears when Columbia University's graduate journalism school didn't immediately admit me. Now, many years later, I would have an exalted seat at the table within Pulitzer Hall inside the Columbia Journalism School.

In early 2012, I thought that being the first woman editor of my hometown daily and a member of the Pulitzer Prize board would be my most notable professional accomplishments. Both were beyond what I had dared to hope for. And now that I was over fifty, I assumed that I knew perfectly well what the first lines of my obituary would say. But life was about to take a radical turn.

3

Pulling Up Roots

I was driving on Chapin Parkway, the leafy Olmsted-designed boulevard near my house in Buffalo, when a phone number flashed onto the dashboard display: (212) 556-1234. "Margaret, this is Arthur Sulzberger," came the disembodied voice. I pulled over to the curb. For weeks—or, if you looked at it another way, for years—I had been waiting for this moment, and I preferred not to commemorate it by smashing my car into a tree. The publisher of *The New York Times* was about to offer me the job that had been created a decade earlier after a combination of scandals (a rogue reporter's fabrications and the misleading reporting in the run-up to the Iraq War) had caused the leadership at the newspaper to establish some reforms. One of these was to hire an internal critic and reader representative, or in other words, an ombudsman. But the *Times*'s grander title for this position was "public editor." The concept: An experienced, independent-minded journalist would come to work at the paper for a limited period (limited so that this outside perspective didn't become an inside one), in order to hold reporters and editors to high standards and to field complaints from readers. This journalist would investigate when things went wrong, would be given full access to the decision-makers, and would then use that reporting to inform the readership. He or she (it had always been a he) would write about the findings in a column that the *Times* itself would publish. In the years after it was established, the handful of journalists who held the job had brought varying styles to it, some more aggressive or critical than others, some who leaned more heavily on commentary, others who emphasized reporting. Always, though, the *Times* public editor's work drew a great deal of outside attention; it was a high-profile position, to say the least. Some people went so far as to call it "the worst job in journalism," given the big egos and the inherent tension of reporting critically on one's own colleagues. I didn't see it that way. The role had fascinated me ever since the first *Times* public editor, Dan Okrent, started writing his pointed columns in late 2003, and even before that when *The Washington Post*'s various ombudsmen had published their work. Most memorably, at the *Post,* Bill Green wrote a tour de force investigation of reporter Janet Cooke's made-up story about an eight-year-old heroin addict; her feature story won a Pulitzer Prize in 1981 that then had to be ignominiously returned. At my desk in the newsroom of the *Buffalo News,* I had read Okrent's columns hungrily, and with a growing sense of a calling. When I read the news that the fourth public editor, Arthur Brisbane, would be finishing his tenure and that the position would be open, I decided to pursue it and did so aggressively, diving into the application process with a single-minded focus. I really wanted the job, in part because I was itching for a life and career change, and in part because I thought that being the public editor of *The New York Times* was something I would be good at. I knew I was smart, had good judgment, and would not be afraid of evaluating the journalism at a big national paper. I certainly had plenty of experience. Three decades of reporting, editing, and leading an urban newsroom had provided that. Over the past twelve years as editor, I had steered the paper through lawsuits from angry businessmen claiming defamation or libel, without ever settling or losing a case. I had dealt with community complaints about racist news coverage, and agreed with some of them, admitting error and putting reforms in place. And I had made consequential judgments on what news to publish and how to present it to our readers—for example, whether to honor a defense lawyer's objections over when to publish the jailhouse confession of his client James Kopp, regarding the murder of abortion provider Barnett Slepian. (We published the confession on our schedule, not his.) In other words, I felt ready.

On that phone call, I asked Sulzberger about the salary, something that hadn't come up in my various interviews for the public editor job over the past two months. After all, I would be moving to a much more expensive city, had a daughter in college and a son in law school, and after a twenty-year marriage, I'd been through a draining divorce. "Don't worry about that," he responded, and I pictured him in his thirteenth-floor office, high above the fray of Midtown Manhattan, dismissing my salary question with a magnanimous wave of the hand. (In fact, it took some negotiating later with the *Times*'s budget-keepers to match and even improve upon my executive editor's salary, but I had Sulzberger's airy promise to remind them of, and that carried considerable weight. I got what I asked for.) But, in the moment, his specific response about money really didn't matter; I was prepared to accept. In the dappled sunshine of that summer day in 2012, sitting in my parked car, I told Sulzberger I'd take the job. It had happened. I would be the fifth public editor of *The New York Times,* and the first woman.

I went home to start dismantling my life to prepare for the move to New York. Within a day or so, a crick developed in the left side of my neck, reaching down into my left shoulder. Having run a robust newsroom while raising young children, I had experienced plenty of stress and anxiety in my life. The scheduling conflicts and adrenaline rushes never stopped, and I had shouldered a lot of responsibility. But now, as I moved to the *Times* to take on this new role, the stakes were higher. Would I be up to the journalistic challenges ahead? Could I even manage to sell my house and get rid of all the accumulated possessions of having lived for decades in one city? By the time I reported for duty at 620 Eighth Avenue a few weeks later, the shoulder pain and I had settled into a long-term relationship. It was part of the price of this adventure, this chance for a growth spurt in middle age, and I was more than willing to pay it.

Within weeks, I had rented an apartment in the Flatiron District, three times as expensive as the monthly mortgage I had been paying in Buffalo. But I could walk to the *Times* from there, or take a short subway ride, and I had a spectacular view of the Empire State Building just a few blocks north. The constant, dominant presence of that Art Deco skyscraper, lit with different symbolic colors each night, began to seem personal—almost familial—and I would introduce the building to visiting friends as "my uncle." I arrived in the city on Labor Day weekend, arranged a few things in my new space, and rode my bicycle to Central Park, where I gazed at the lake and felt a spiritual connection with the New York writers I loved, some from the past, others very much alive and living right on this island with me: Anna Quindlen, Toni Morrison, E. B. White, James Baldwin, Nora Ephron, J. D. Salinger, Joan Didion, David Halberstam, Gay Talese. I was thrilled, and I also felt curiously at home. I once again read E. B. White's classic essay "Here Is New York," published in 1949, and smiled at one of its first lines: "No one should come to New York to live unless he is willing to be lucky."

A few days later, I was in a fired-up mood for my first day at work as I walked into the Renzo Piano–designed skyscraper with its transparent walls, glass-enclosed garden, and multilevel newsroom, lined with exposed staircases where editors would gather the staff to celebrate their endless Pulitzer Prizes. An editorial assistant showed me to my office on the third floor, not far from the obituary writers, which may have been a subtle statement about my status in the newsroom. My desk was piled with boxes of freshly printed stationery and business cards featuring my name and my new title on ivory stock with black letters in the *Times*'s distinctive font. But I would barely touch them in the years ahead. Unlike the four previous public editors, I would be doing the job mostly online.

I started off by tweeting to my four hundred followers (I had joined Twitter less than a year before) something about being dedicated to serving the readers of the *Times*. In retrospect, this was far too earnest a tone for snarky Twitter; a friend had suggested I simply tweet: "The public editor is in the house." That would have been immeasurably cooler. And I settled down to write my first post on the *Public Editor's Journal* blog. I wanted to set the tone for my stint by advocating for rigorous adherence not just to the facts but to the truth, and away from the defensive, performative neutrality that some were beginning to call false balance or false equivalence ("Some say the earth is round; others insist it is flat" or, more pertinent, "Some say climate change is real and caused partly by human behavior; others insist it doesn't exist"). Before the day was over and just before my post was published on the *Times* website, my twenty-five-year-old assistant, Joseph Burgess, who had been the assistant to the last public editor, saved me from an embarrassing error. He popped in to ask me a question as he prepared to put my post into the content-management system for publication. He wanted to know if I was sure that *Times* reporter Michael Cooper, whom I had described as being at the Democratic National Convention, was really still in Charlotte. I realized that was only my assumption after interviewing Cooper by phone, and removed the reference to his location. Later that day, I saw the reporter right there in the New York newsroom, and chatted with him in a hallway. Burgess, bless him, had prevented me from having to append a correction to my first piece of public editor writing. It wouldn't be the last time that my young assistants—five of them would hold the role during my stint—would prove their worth.

I soon found out that anything written in *The New York Times* gets an immense response. Immediately after my initial blog post went online, media writers criticized or praised me, a press ethics expert called to disagree with what I'd written, and hundreds of readers responded in the blog's comments section, by email, and on Twitter. The topic of avoiding false equivalency, pegged to the convention where Barack Obama was being nominated for reelection, had clearly hit a nerve. One commenter wrote: "I sincerely hope Ms. Sullivan is serious when she asks, 'What is the role of the media if not to press for some semblance of reality amid the smoke and mirrors?' and will use her position to push the media to do this job. There's a whole lot of smoke to clear." People seemed to like the direction I was taking and the brisk pace I was keeping, responding to issues in real time.

When *New York* magazine put "The Rapturous Reception of Margaret Sullivan" into a headline and wrote that I had "gained something of an Internet fan club" after one month on the job, I began to think that this might turn out to be fun. Still, my neck and shoulder tension hadn't gone away. For good reason: The inherent difficulty of the job—being an outsider with inside access, complete independence, and a big platform—made itself known quickly a few days later when I met with a group of senior *Times* editors. With the purpose of getting to know me, about twenty editors, mostly white men (with a few notable exceptions), gathered in a big conference room, the same place where they made consequential decisions every day about which articles and photographs deserved to be on the front page. Jill Abramson, the first woman to run the newsroom as executive editor, was sitting in one of the grass-green swivel chairs that were placed around the gleaming table. So was her second-in-command, Dean Baquet. The standards editor, Phil Corbett, was there, as was his deputy, Greg Brock, who was in charge of correcting errors. So were the heads of Metro, National, and other sections. The group was welcoming, even friendly. But I noticed a tense undercurrent. Fully aware that I could make their lives miserable if I called out their misjudgments or errors, some seemed eager to let me know they wouldn't be pushed around by an unknown editor from a place that many of them could not have pointed to on the map. (Even though Buffalo is the second-largest city in the state, at holiday time I was often asked by well-meaning *Times* people if I would be "heading up north," as if I were going to Montreal; a map of New York State suggests that my route was mostly west.) The culture editor, Jonathan Landman, asked me a question that brought a hush to the room: "Did *you* have an ombudsman when you were the editor in Buffalo?" And when he followed up with "Why not?" I stumbled, explaining that I had tried to be an accessible chief editor, quick to respond directly to reader complaints, so an ombudsman wasn't needed. This seemed to satisfy no one. Another editor asked what subjects I expected to concentrate on, and someone called out, "Anonymous sources, right?"—suggesting that I would probably join my predecessors in criticizing how much the *Times* allowed government officials to get out their message without the accountability of having their names attached. Knowing how much the paper had hurt its own credibility in the past because of this overused practice, I agreed that that was a good bet.

The editors were clearly trying to get a handle on how I would approach the job, how tough I planned to be, whether I would treat them fairly and understand their decision-making. They asked me which of the paper's previous public editors, in my opinion, had done the best job. A couple of them pointedly put forward the name of *their* favorite: Clark Hoyt, the former Washington bureau chief for the Knight-Ridder newspaper chain, who had held the public editor job a few years earlier. I agreed that I admired Hoyt's thorough and fair-minded reporting. When I mentioned my admiration for Okrent, who had been particularly fearless as well as an elegant writer, I got some sour looks. (Okrent was remembered particularly for writing a column in 2004 that posed the rhetorical question of whether the *Times* was a liberal newspaper, and answering memorably at the top of his column: "Of course it is.") After about an hour, the grilling was over—none too soon for me.

On that late summer day in 2012, I had plenty of worries about the news business. I had spent the last several years cutting the newsroom budget at *The Buffalo News,* mostly by offering buyouts to veteran reporters and editors; the staff of 200 was down to 140 by the time I left. That was painful because, after my three decades at the paper, many of these journalists felt like family members to me, and because I knew very well that a smaller staff meant we couldn't do as much reporting on the city and region we served. This was true not just on hard-news topics; when our full-time theater critic retired, for example, we combined the roles of drama and art critic, but we still had a crack movie critic, Jeff Simon, who doubled as the books editor, and two music critics in Jeff Miers and Mary Kunz, both of whom I had hired. After the announcement that I would be leaving Buffalo for the *Times,* lots of people asked me if I felt guilty, as if I were a captain deserting her ship. The answer was simple: I didn't. I had given my hometown paper three decades of my life and career, had done my best, and was fully ready to move on.

When the 2008 recession hit, the *Times* went through the same kind of newsroom cost-cutting, reducing its much larger staff through buyouts and layoffs while trying to figure out how to make up for the loss of print advertising revenue that had long been the paper's lifeblood. It was a tough time for newspapers, big and small. I worried about that.

But one thing I wasn't too concerned about was whether

most Americans *believed* the news, whether they trusted the essential truth of what they read and heard from the mainstream press. Granted, trust had declined sharply since the 1970s. Soon after the Watergate scandal and the publication of the Pentagon Papers, when public trust was at its height, Americans seemed to feel that the national press was doing its watchdog role, keeping powerful people and institutions accountable. But over the next several decades, many factors would come along that—fairly or not—began to slice away at that positive feeling and that sense of trust. Some of this was the fault of journalists and news organizations themselves, and some of it was the result of outside forces. A perception of liberal bias, coupled with well-publicized ethical failures like the *Post*'s Janet Cooke disaster, caused Americans to feel that the national media was out of touch with their concerns. This was fed by relentless criticism from conservative politicians, from Nixon to Newt Gingrich; they fanned the flames of mistrust, as did the bashing from right-wing pundits like Rush Limbaugh on the radio or Bill O'Reilly on Fox News, which had been founded in 1996 and called itself "fair and balanced," but which was actually meant to help the conservative cause and to make billions by stirring up public outrage. Practices like the overuse of anonymous sources, especially prevalent in the flawed reporting about supposed weapons of mass destruction that helped lead America into the disastrous Iraq War, made things even worse. There were plenty of warning signs of this declining trust: charges of blatant media bias, anger at the *Times* and other mainstream news outlets for being leftist, legitimate disgust over the reporting in the run-up to war. The storm was building. In 2012, though, as I began settling into my new job, the level of Americans' basic trust in the news—in truth itself—didn't feel to me like anything close to a full-blown disaster. But over time, from my front-row seat at *The New York Times,* I would watch the crisis develop. I would do what I could, at this powerful institution, to fend it off.

4

"Welcome to the Fishbowl"

A scientist named Yvonne Brill had died, and the *Times*, in its wisdom, had decided she was worthy of an obituary. That was the normal part. The not-so-normal part happened almost as soon as the obituary was posted online. Brill was a rocket scientist with remarkable accomplishments, but the obituary's first paragraph focused on her domestic life, and its second paragraph seemed to mention her professional achievements almost an afterthought. It began like this:

> She made a mean beef stroganoff, followed her husband from job to job and took eight years off from work to raise three children. "The world's best mom," her son Matthew said.
>
> But Yvonne Brill, who died on Wednesday at 88 in Princeton, N.J., was also a brilliant rocket scientist who in the early 1970s invented a propulsion system to keep communications satellites from slipping out of their orbits.

Well before the obituary appeared in the printed newspaper, the Twitter universe was ablaze with mocking criticism of the *Times* for writing the obit in a way that downplayed Brill's scientific work. Some were angry, calling it outright sexism: Would any official account of a man's life read this way? Others were sardonically entertained and wanted to propose the cooking accomplishments they would like included in the first line of *their* obituary. "Dear NYT, just in case you're pre-writing obits of obscure book critics, everybody says I make delicious chocolate chip cookies," tweeted *The Washington Post*'s book critic Ron Charles.

When I interviewed the obituaries editor, William McDonald, he made it clear that he didn't see why there was a problem. As he explained it, the early references to cooking and being a mother served as an effective setup for the "aha!" of the second paragraph, which revealed that Brill was an important scientist. "I'm surprised," he told me. "It never occurred to us that this would be read as sexist." And the writer of the obit, Douglas Martin, saw the negative reaction as unwarranted, the whining of shallow people who didn't read the obituary fully but reacted only to what they saw on Twitter about the opening paragraph. It hadn't changed his mind about how he wrote it. Even after all the criticism, he told me, "I wouldn't do anything differently."

Martin was upset, though, at being attacked online, and he vented his anger in heated tones as he sat in my office—only a few yards from his desk—giving me an on-the-record response that I would use in a blog post. McDonald and Martin, both of whom I had had some pleasant conversations with since starting the job a few months earlier, seemed to think I should be defending them against what they saw as the Twitter mob. I got the feeling that they wanted me to use my column to explain and justify their decisions. The problem was that I didn't agree with their thinking, as I wrote in my post. After quoting the critics, as well as McDonald and Martin, and noting that the online version of the obituary was edited before it published in print to address the complaints (the beef stroganoff reference disappeared entirely), I ended the post like this:

> Here's my take: It was fine for the obituary to point out how unusual it was for a woman to be a successful rocket scientist at midcentury and what the obstacles were.
>
> And the way she handled her role as a wife and mother certainly had a place, given the era in which she did her work. Cultural context is important.
>
> But if Yvonne Brill's life was worth writing about because of her achievements, and all agree that it was, then the glories of her beef stroganoff should have been little more than a footnote.
>
> The emphasis on her domesticity—and, more important, the obituary's overall framing as a story about gender—had the effect of undervaluing what really landed Mrs. Brill on the Times obituaries page: her groundbreaking scientific work.

In some ways, the Yvonne Brill dustup was, as I acknowledged in my post, "a tempest in a Crock-pot"—certainly not an earth-shattering matter. It wasn't even in the top one hundred controversies I had to deal with. It was a telling episode, though, because it featured so many of the elements that would characterize my stint as public editor: Intense criticism that began on Twitter. Defensive reaction from the *Times.* Discomfort for me because of the physical proximity to the journalists whose work I was criticizing. And, in general, appreciation from the readership. Of course, not everyone agreed with my conclusions, but people did seem to like that I had taken up the mini-controversy immediately and conducted what they considered a fair-minded and thorough job of dealing with a complaint. To use my own regular tagline, here's my take on the Yvonne Brill episode: It was just another stressful day at the office. Not only stressful but very, very visible. "Welcome to the fishbowl," was *Times* spokeswoman Eileen Murphy's greeting when I began the job; she certainly had that correct.

In nearly four years in the job, I never had a completely comfortable day as public editor. If the people I worked next to were happy with me, I felt guilty for being too soft on the institution. (This didn't happen often.) If they were upset with me—sometimes even furious—I felt besieged and worried that I had made the wrong judgment or had been too harsh. If I hadn't written anything in a couple of days, I felt like a slacker since there were hundreds of reader emails to deal with every week. Thankfully, I didn't take the first cut at these endless complaints; that triage fell to a series of young "confidential assistants" who were assigned to me for roughly a year apiece; each one of them—Joseph Burgess, Meghan Gourley, Jonah Bromwich, Joumana Khatib, and Evan Gershkovich—was excellent and invaluable. Time after time, they saved me from mistakes, served as sounding boards, and suggested which subjects seemed to need taking up most urgently.

From the beginning, I pushed myself to give this singular job all of my energy and the best judgment I could muster. I knew what I had to offer: an outsider's perspective, my background as a top editor, and a clear sense of journalistic right and wrong. At times, I felt like Nick Carraway in *The Great Gatsby*—the visitor from the Midwest who had come east and so was able to observe the scene from an outsider's perspective. I took comfort in knowing that, unlike almost everyone at the *Times,* I had run a newsroom, albeit a smaller one. At *The Buffalo News,* for nearly thirteen years, my desk was where the buck stopped on unending problems and challenges. These included public-records fights with Buffalo's mayor and police chief, demands (often reasonable and constructive ones) from the union representing our journalists to change working conditions, and pressure from the publisher to tinker with stories he was personally involved with. I had dealt with all of this and so much more. With the help of the newsroom management team I had assembled and whose counsel I often sought, I had survived them all. When I arrived at the *Times,* I may have questioned myself or felt insecure occasionally, but underneath all of that, I had a sense of confidence that I knew a thing or two. At a deep level I trusted my own judgment and my own gut. Still, it could be a challenging situation, sometimes close to impossible. The *Times* newsroom was packed with reporters and editors who, having reached the starry heights of their profession, were not always inclined to be open to constructive criticism, especially when delivered publicly.

One of my first tests came with the Tesla controversy, which pitted the *Times*'s automotive journalists against Elon Musk, the billionaire entrepreneur and CEO of the famous electric car company, and his many devotees who felt he could do no wrong. The problem began with *Times* writer John Broder's test drive of the Model S Tesla and the company's new super-charging stations, which were supposed to allow Tesla owners to make long-distance trips. Broder's test drive, to put it mildly, didn't go well: The Model S ran out of juice along the way. "Stalled Out on Tesla's Electric Highway" read the headline of the test-drive story, accompanied by a color photo of the cherry-red car being transported, after the failed test, on a flatbed truck. The story was a black eye for Tesla—one that Musk had no interest in accepting with equanimity. The CEO hit back hard: The story was faked, he claimed, and Broder intentionally caused the car to fail. On his blog, Musk laid out the evidence, as he saw it, using the Model S's computer-generated driving logs. Broder and his editors couldn't really counter those claims effectively, since the reporter had merely taken conventional notes in a small notebook that sat next to him on the front seat. It amounted to conventional journalism going up against advanced technology.

Besieged by aggrieved Elon Musk superfans on one side and worried *Times* journalists on the other—and lacking a great deal of automotive expertise myself—I spent days investigating and trying to come to a conclusion. When I did, it made news in a number of publications, as my pronouncements often did. "*New York Times* Public Editor Margaret Sullivan has published her final word on the *New York Times* vs. Tesla saga, saying she does not think writer John M. Broder purposefully sabotaged the Model S test drive. But she isn't letting him off the hook completely," wrote Rebecca Greenfield in *The Atlantic*. The test drive was done in good faith, I concluded—I saw no reason to question Broder's journalistic integrity—but the reporter didn't use the best judgment along the way, which didn't help the car's performance. Nor was he precise enough in compiling his evidence of the drive's failures; that lack of precision left him and the *Times* vulnerable to attack.

The Tesla controversy was, at some level, unimportant. It centered on a test drive, after all, not a national security breach. But readers cared, some of them passionately, and I knew in my gut that anything that brought criticism of the paper's integrity had to be taken seriously. Still, there were far more consequential problems than obituaries and electric cars, ones that went to the heart of the paper's credibility and mission. Others touched on sensitive issues of race that were roiling newsrooms across the country as old-school practices and thinking ran up against the beliefs of a new generation steeped in the values of diversity, equity, and inclusion.

I agreed, for example, with readers who were outraged by television critic Alessandra Stanley's 2014 piece that opened with a racist trope: "When Shonda Rhimes writes her autobiography, it should be called 'How to Get Away with Being an Angry Black Woman.'" In the same article, Stanley referred to Viola Davis as "less classically beautiful" than other Black actresses; that phrase quickly became a mocking hashtag. After blaming Twitter for the viral blowback, Stanley told me that she had assumed her loyal readers would understand. "I didn't think *Times* readers would take the opening sentence literally," she said, "because I so often write arch, provocative ledes that are then undercut or mitigated by the paragraphs that follow." I didn't quite buy that, and privately thought that "arch, provocative ledes" might make a pretty good hashtag, too. More broadly, the episode gave me the opportunity to write about the importance of newsroom diversity and to point out that of the paper's twenty culture critics at that time, not one was Black.

One of the most stressful episodes came in 2015 when a talented young *Times* reporter, Sarah Maslin Nir, published her fascinating two-part investigation about the employee abuse rampant within New York City's hundreds of nail salons, many of which were owned and staffed by immigrants from China and Korea. Workers sometimes had their wages stolen by salon owners, and were constantly exposed to dangerous chemicals. The series, called "Unvarnished," hit like a bomb when it was published, thanks to an elaborate *Times* rollout similar to a high-end book launch. The praise for Nir's enterprising reporting, which had taken her more than thirteen months, was widespread and effusive. "This is why we need the *New York Times*. Thank you," wrote one commenter, with five hundred others chiming in to agree. Immediately, the project brought about governmental reform at the state level and was mentioned as a strong contender for a Pulitzer Prize, recognition that is extremely important at the *Times*. Soon, though, doubts arose about some of the investigation's conclusions. A former *Times* reporter, Richard Bernstein, who, along with his wife and sister-in-law, both originally from China, owned nail salons in the city, published a lengthy critique of Nir's reporting in a somewhat unlikely place, *The New York Review of Books*. Bernstein got in touch with me, too, wanting me to write my own critique that might amplify some of his points: that Nir's conclusions were overstated, that the salon employee abuses, while real, were not as widespread as depicted, and that some characterizations in the series were simply wrong. He used fighting words like "flimsy" and "wholly inaccurate."

Executive editor Dean Baquet had issued a persuasive point-by-point rebuttal, but I knew I had to take up the subject; it was far too hot to ignore. I also knew that what I would say would probably carry a lot of weight because of the intense disagreement and the high stakes. I felt like a referee at a cage fight. I interviewed many of the players; at one surreal point, two metro desk editors sat in my office as one of them, Michael Luo, translated into English Chinese-language classified advertisements for salon employees from neighborhood newspapers. What I ended up writing didn't fully absolve the *Times* of the outside criticism. I admired the investigation but called it overwrought in places and said that one piece of evidence of ridiculously low wages was overstated. The series probably needed to be dialed back about 10 percent before being published, seldom a bad idea with a big investigation. My conclusions didn't make me many friends on the staff. But then again, that's not what I was there for. (The investigation ended up as a Pulitzer finalist, but not a winner.)

What made criticizing the project even harder was that Nir had made efforts to cultivate, even befriend, me early in my tenure. She asked me to come speak to a group of young

Times women who called themselves the Old Girls Club and who got together occasionally to support each other's careers. They sought the advice of other experienced women journalists, including Gail Collins, the op-ed columnist and former *Times* editorial page editor. One day after work, on Nir's invitation, I met the young women—mostly reporters in their twenties—at Smith's, a bar on Eighth Avenue. I listened as they went through their regular opening ritual of going around the table and unapologetically bragging about some recent accomplishment; the exercise was supposed to overcome women's tendency to downplay their own strengths. Afterward, they asked me questions about how I had managed my own career and whether I had encountered sexism along the way.

That was all very flattering; these young women already were far ahead of where I had been at their age, just by virtue of having landed at the *Times*. So when I criticized Nir's "Unvarnished" investigation, I had the feeling of betraying the young sisterhood that had reached out to me. I reminded myself, though, that I hadn't come to the *Times* to be a mentor or a friend. I was there as the readers' representative and an internal critic. I gave Nir plenty of credit in my column for the virtues of her investigation, writing that the series "effectively and movingly does some of the core work of journalism: It gives voice to the voiceless, and by illuminating wrongdoing and suffering, it advocates for those who cannot do so for themselves." I couldn't find it faultless, however, no matter how much I might have liked its author personally.

Despite the seriousness of the job, I tried to have some fun along the way. Because I wrote an almost-daily blog, not just a weekly or bimonthly print column, I gave myself the freedom to take a lighter approach once in a while. I started a series of posts called "Perfectly Reasonable Questions," asking a *Times* editor to answer a query from a reader. For example, in 2015, I asked standards editor Phil Corbett to expound on whether the paper should quote public officials directly when it was really their public relations people providing the quotes in a written statement; Corbett urged transparency in the writing. At the end of each of those posts, I encouraged readers to send me other questions but noted—I hoped humorously—that *I* would be the one to decide what was perfectly reasonable.

When the Styles section published stories revealing dubious fashion or lifestyle trends (granny underwear, man buns, colorfully dyed underarm hair), I joined those in the reading audience who found them ridiculous. The silliness reached a peak with an amusing but far-fetched story about the supposed popularity of wearing a monocle as a fashion accessory (headline: "One Part Mr. Peanut, One Part Hipster Chic"), and this gave birth to my own whimsical invention, the Monocle Meter. In a blog post, I asked readers to contribute stories to be rated with 1 to 10 monocles: "Send me your goofy trends, your ridiculous interviews, your fatuous features, yearning to be mocked." In subsequent posts, I assigned monocle ratings, something like rating movies with varying numbers of popcorn boxes. By that point, my location in the newsroom had been shifted from near the obituaries desk to a place right within Styles, bringing me full circle to my days running the Life & Arts section in Buffalo. The section editor, Stuart Emmrich, was only one office away, and writers like Katie Rosman, Alex Williams, Jacob Bernstein, and Alexandra Jacobs had desks nearby. I saw them all every day, and they were good-natured about the ribbing I was giving to some of their pieces.

When the legendary media columnist David Carr died suddenly in early 2015, I attended his packed funeral at St. Ignatius Loyola Church on Park Avenue. After, I shared a cab across Central Park, back to the *Times* office, with Katie Rosman, who had come to the paper from *The Wall Street Journal* and, like many others, was devastated by Carr's loss. He had mentored her and a host of other young journalists. Moved by the ceremony and the eulogies, we talked about David and about our own lives and our families. Much as I enjoyed Rosman's engaging company and admired her work, I felt wary about becoming too friendly. I always had to keep myself a bit apart; I couldn't afford to become an insider or to feel that there were people whom I wouldn't want to criticize if the occasion should arise. Not being able to make friends at work was part of the isolation and inherent tension of the job. I told myself that it was a good thing that I had made lots of friends earlier in my life and career; I wasn't adding any at the *Times*.

Some staffers made it easy to keep my distance. I had no interest, for instance, in becoming friends with the sports editor, Jason Stallman, one of the few people at the *Times* who seemed to have little appreciation of the public editor's role and who was unusually defensive about even my mildest criticism. When I agreed with readers who wanted the *Times* to pay more attention to women's sports, especially college basketball, he made it clear that he found it ridiculous that I had mentioned in a post that I had played basketball in high school and college and so had particular interest in the topic myself.

A bigger disturbance with Stallman arose over a story that the sports department saw fit to do about tennis superstar Serena Williams's body type. It was published during the 2015 Wimbledon tournament and just before her championship win. I started hearing angry criticism of the story, which carried the headline "Tennis's Top Women Balance Body Image with Ambition." The idea of the story was that despite Serena's remarkable success, some other tennis players had decided not to emulate her power game by becoming more muscular. For example, it quoted the coach of Agnieszka Radwanska: "It's our decision to keep her as the smallest player in the top 10. Because first of all she's a woman and wants to be a woman." The feminist writer Roxanne Gay tweeted: "That NY Times story on Serena's body is so misguided and racist and utter trash." I decided to write about it, quoting the critics and interviewing its author, the well-respected freelance writer Ben Rothenberg, as well as Stallman.

My post was critical of the piece but not harshly so: It gave both of them their say in defending it. I knew that Rothenberg felt remorseful about presenting the ingrained societal ideas about ideal women's bodies as a given and not sufficiently challenging them. I knew he was stunned by the vociferous criticism that was coming his way. That couldn't have been easy. Stallman seemed much more self-satisfied, though both of them acknowledged that the story could have been better. It was just another day at the office until I heard about what Stallman had told an interviewer for *The Takeaway*, a program on WNYC, the New York City public radio station, who had asked him not only about public reaction to the story but also about my fault-finding. Insisting that it was absurd to see the article as the *Times* taking a position on the subject of women's body types, he was not only dismissive but disrespectful. Regarding my view that the story was a missed opportunity to dig deeper into why such stereotypes exist and to challenge them, Stallman had this to say: "The public editor's piece was met with a lot of laughter and eyebrow-raising in the newsroom." He was still digging through the emails from his colleagues making fun of my absurd stance, he said. Some radio listeners felt like I did about this; one of them, Ann McIndoo, copied me on a letter to the editor she had written, one that was never published. "Your paper employs an editor who seems to think that since female athletes were interviewed for the article, that the author and the paper have essentially no responsibility for conveying sexist attitudes and expectations," she wrote. Was Stallman really so ignorant of the role that journalists play in framing issues? she wondered. McIndoo added that "when he shared that he and others had a good laugh over the public editor's feedback, I was stunned. To err is human; to laugh off the feedback of your public editor (and the public at large) is unforgivably arrogant."

Stallman seemed to be a popular, well-respected editor at the *Times,* and he's undoubtedly smart and skilled. But the episode left a bad taste in my mouth. When we spoke in person, he was perfectly polite, but in these public remarks, Stallman's behavior was unseemly—whatever his private feelings may have been or how much fun he was having sneering with his colleagues. All of this ran against the whole idea of the constructive role that the public editor was supposed to play.

For the most part, though, even those editors and reporters whose work I put a critical spotlight on were accepting, sometimes even appreciative. The columnist Joe Nocera actually thanked me after I rapped him for factual errors in a column about the famed investor Warren Buffett. (I had to disclose, in my column, that I had worked for Buffett, who owned *The Buffalo News* during my time there.) It couldn't have been fun for Nocera when various publications wrote pieces about my criticism, like one in Politico that carried the headline "Times Public Editor Comes Down Hard on Joe Nocera." But he handled it with grace, publicly admitted his error, and treated it as an opportunity to learn something.

The *Times*'s top editors—Jill Abramson, Dean Baquet, Joe Kahn, Lydia Polgreen, Susan Chira, Carolyn Ryan, Matt Purdy, and Andy Rosenthal—were generally cooperative with me and thoughtful about the issues I raised, if not always pleased with my conclusions. Those in the standards department, Phil Corbett and his deputy, Greg Brock (who calmly litigated the endless flood of demands for corrections), were particularly supportive—though, again, not always in agreement with my judgments. Corbett and Brock had roles that were somewhat similar to mine, in that they dealt with questions of accuracy and journalistic practices, but they were part of the newsroom hierarchy, reporting up to the executive editor, while the public editor was an external role; I was paid by the *Times* but was intended to be independent of the newsroom pecking order. I came to know all of these editors well, as day after day I fielded complaints, asked for their responses, and wrote my posts. I had access to them all; if I asked questions, I got answers. In general, the relationships were cordial. Over time, though, there certainly were some unpleasant disagreements. I seldom felt good about dishing out tough criticism; maybe to a fault, I could put myself in the place of the writers and editors. I could empathize, and at the same time I wanted to be as straightforward in my judgments as possible. I thought that the readers deserved that.

Throughout my tenure, just as senior editors had predicted when I first met with them, I was tough on the overuse of anonymous government sources by *Times* reporters, especially in the reporting from the Washington bureau. You would have thought that the paper finally would have learned its lesson about this after the embarrassment and damage caused by its reporting in the lead-up to the United States' invasion of Iraq in 2003. Reporters, most notably Judith Miller, wrote story after story that led readers to believe that Iraqi leader Saddam Hussein had developed "weapons of mass destruction," which helped to provide a pretext for going to war. That war would prove to be disastrous: extraordinarily deadly, lengthy, and largely pointless. But the stories were based on inaccurate information from unnamed sources in the United States' so-called intelligence community. When it became all too clear that the reporting had been flawed, the *Times* was forced to acknowledge what had happened in a lengthy and blame-accepting editor's note. It said, in essence, that some of these stories had not been reported with sufficient rigor or skepticism, and it pledged to do better.

After that, the newsroom's internal guidelines stated that anonymous sources were to be used rarely—only as "a last resort." My reading of the paper, day after day, suggested that there must have been a tremendous number of last resorts, since attribution to "a U.S. official" or "a Pentagon official" was an extremely common occurrence in the paper.

Readers despised this. The national security reporter Eric Schmitt told me that he had been appointed to a newsroom committee to look into the paper's reporting practices and thus was given access to readership data. Schmitt was surprised to learn that what bothered readers most wasn't factual errors or political bias: "The number one complaint, far and away, was anonymous sources." I constantly heard from readers like David Steinhardt of Hancock, Vermont, who railed against this practice, writing, "I beseech the *Times* not to facilitate government acting like the Wizard of Oz—behind a curtain." He made the point that such reporting "can easily serve to mask unaccountable half-truths and lies." It amounted, in the worst cases, to journalistic stenography, reporting that dutifully records what government officials say without appropriate skepticism or rigorous fact-checking. What's more, because the officials hide behind anonymity, there was no holding them accountable later if their information turned out to be bad.

So, one might ask, if this kind of reporting damaged credibility and if there were guidelines that discouraged it, why on earth did it continue unabated? Bill Hamilton, the national security editor in the Washington bureau and one of the most helpful and reasonable people I encountered, offered an explanation. Because of the Obama administration's crackdown on whistleblowers and on all kinds of leaks to the press, government officials had become even more wary of sharing information with reporters. "It's almost impossible to get people who know anything to talk," Hamilton told me. Getting them to talk on the record is even harder, but news gathering must go on. "So, we're caught in this dilemma."

Then, too, there's the competitive urge, and professional pressure, to break stories, something that's much easier to do when you can offer a source anonymity. This is what's known as "access journalism"—at its worst, a devil's bargain between reporters and their sources, in which each wins but the reader loses.

None of this is simple. Some of the most important journalism of the modern era (*The Washington Post*'s Watergate-scandal reporting, for instance, or Jane Mayer's stunning reporting on the CIA's "black sites") was accomplished, at least partly, through the use of confidential sources. It's a crucial, even indispensable tool in ferreting out information that's important to the public interest—especially when so much government information has been classified, often put in that category unnecessarily. The practice was being vastly overused, though, not just for ultra-sensitive reporting on the national security beat but also for all kinds of frivolous purposes—in gossipy entertainment pieces, in personality profiles, in real estate stories. What's more, the excuses given for relying on it were getting more and more strained, more and more absurd.

I went on a campaign in my blog against unnamed sources. I started an effort I called AnonyWatch, and asked readers to send me examples of anonymous sourcing and so-called blind quotes when they saw them in the paper. Many complied, and every once in a while I'd write a column rounding them up, or I would draw attention to them on Twitter.

Eventually, in early 2015, Matt Gross of *New York* magazine memorialized all of this in a piece titled "On the Condition of Anonymity: A Poem for Margaret Sullivan." It was introduced with a short setup, a passage from one of my recent columns: "For many months now, I've been keeping track of the overuse of anonymous sources in *The Times* as a way of discouraging a practice that readers rightly object to. The practice continues apace—as do ever more inventive reasons for granting anonymity." And then Gross's lengthy poem began, growing ever more bizarre with each free-verse line:

> *In keeping with diplomatic custom, with NATO practice, with a strong Vatican tradition of secrecy, with the peculiar conventions of Oscar publicity—*
> *In order to talk more freely about the campaign's internal thinking*
> *in order to protect her nephew's identity—*
> *To avoid drawing attention at her school*
> *to avoid upsetting past and potential future employers*
> *to avoid possible conflict with fellow executives in a rapidly changing situation*
> *to avoid antagonizing law enforcement officials*
> *to avoid disciplinary measures from the White House . . .*

The list went on for dozens more lines before its anticlimactic words: "He spoke."

The poem was clever and funny, and in every detail all too

realistic. Far from being treated as a last resort, anonymity was being handed out as generously as Snickers bars on Halloween. Eventually I would make some headway in getting the *Times* to change its ingrained bad habits on unnamed sourcing, habits that were so damaging to public trust. But it would take a journalistic disaster to make that happen.

5

But Her Emails . . .

The New York Times has long prided itself on being the definitive news source. "All the News That's Fit to Print" is its longtime motto for good reason: The paper (whether in digital or print form) aims to be the first and last word on the tidings of the day. But how prominently a story is covered in *The New York Times,* the language in the headline, the framing given to a revelation or controversy—it all sets the tone for the way the larger news ecosystem, from the TV networks to social media, reacts. That's especially true in the first twenty-four hours after a big story breaks; it's been the case for a long time and remains so today. The Hillary Clinton coverage was particularly consequential.

The *Times*'s coverage of Clinton seemed puzzling from the moment I started paying close attention to it in my first months as public editor. It took me a long time and a lot of thought—and plenty of complaints from *Times* readers—to figure out what felt wrong about the coverage. I kept trying to analyze the problem in a binary way. Was it too positive, too glowing? That didn't seem to be the case. Or was it too negative, seemingly intent on tearing her down? That wasn't really it either. Eventually I was able to put my finger on it—and to write a public editor column about it. There would be many more such Clinton-focused columns to follow, right up until I finished my stint at the *Times* in 2016, about six months before she lost the presidential election. Some of these columns would find their way into her 2017 book, *What Happened,* published after that crushing loss to Donald Trump, as she and many other Americans tried to grapple with that pressing question. Of course, there were many factors that resulted in Trump's victory, including the growing intolerance toward racial minorities in some parts of the country, the seeming inability of Democrats to articulate a vision that Americans could latch on to, and Clinton's flawed campaign, which nonetheless gave her a significant edge in the popular vote. But the media overall certainly played an important role, and like everyone else, Clinton clearly understood the power of *The New York Times,* which explained her book's inclusion of what a newspaper ombudswoman had written about her.

The implied question in her book's title was apt. What *had* happened in a campaign that was supposed to smoothly deliver her to the Oval Office as the first woman president? Almost everyone thought she would win—even Trump himself. The *Times,* because of its great influence, surely was one of the factors. When I hear people complaining about the supposedly liberal mainstream media, I like to remind them that it was *The New York Times* that broke the story about Hillary Clinton's emails and pursued it aggressively and, earlier, raised questions about the Clinton Foundation that gave a great deal of fuel to her opponents.

The reason the *Times*/Hillary problem (as I saw it) wasn't

obvious was that there was a confounding paradox at its heart. On the one hand, the campaign coverage treated her as the obvious next president. At times it felt like the prelude to a coronation. On the other hand, the coverage, which set out to be tough-minded, ended up also being extremely damaging, sometimes beyond what was reasonable.

In 2013—well before Clinton had even declared her candidacy for the Democratic nomination—executive editor Jill Abramson assigned a talented and fast-rising staffer who had been covering the news media, Amy Chozick, to report on Clinton full-time, although the beat was defined more broadly. That is, Chozick was to cover Hillary *and* the whole world of the Clintons writ large. But, in essence, this assignment meant that Chozick would focus largely on the would-be candidate. I interviewed her and her editor, Carolyn Ryan, soon after she was assigned to the beat, and soon after I started hearing from *Times* readers about their objections.

Chozick was forthcoming as she sat in my office, talking engagingly about her new assignment. In our conversation, which was on the record, she made it clear that she felt significant pressure from above to produce scoops and other coverage that *Times* competitors wouldn't have. Her editors, including Abramson, had told her to "own" the Clinton beat. Consequently, Chozick told me, "I live in constant fear" of losing even a single Clinton story to another news organization. And Ryan, a high-ranking editor who had been the *Times* Washington bureau chief and now was the senior editor for politics coverage, explained to me why there was such emphasis on Hillary Clinton at such an early stage. With Obama set to finish his second term, the *Times* leadership viewed Clinton, who was then secretary of state (and, of course, a former senator and First Lady), as "the closest thing we have to an incumbent" in the 2016 election. Ryan told me what the paper hoped to accomplish with this early coverage: "With the Clintons, there is a certain opacity and stagecraft and silly coverage elsewhere [but] Amy can penetrate a lot of that."

I always found Ryan, who had come to the *Times* from *The Boston Globe,* approachable; unlike some of her colleagues, she seemed to understand that we often wouldn't be in agreement, but she rolled with the punches, and any disagreement never lingered. Her outgoing personality served as a counterbalance to her ambition and finely tuned sense of internal politics. Almost as soon as I arrived as public editor, she suggested we go out to lunch. We walked over to Sardi's, that theater district standby of old New York, where she quizzed me relentlessly about my background, family, and journalistic views. I felt as if she were interviewing me, but it wasn't unpleasant; instead it seemed to arise both from her natural curiosity, certainly a good quality in any journalist, and—maybe, I thought—from a desire to protect herself in the future. Know thy enemy?

The all-in approach to covering Clinton at this early stage seemed ill-advised to me, as well as to some of the most astute observers I knew in journalism. I interviewed and quoted some of them for my column. Tom Rosenstiel, head of the American Press Institute and a former *Los Angeles Times* media critic, told me he doubted if it really was wise to "perpetuate the permanent campaign." He meant the kind of incessant national politics that never takes a year off but just keeps rolling. Brendan Nyhan, a political scientist at

Dartmouth College, pointedly wondered if a full-time Clinton beat would "cement the perception that she is the inevitable Democratic nominee and effectively serve to pre-anoint her."

As usual, these kinds of concerns, once aired in my column, didn't seem to penetrate the *Times*'s confident decision-making. Many readers, though, did seem to agree with these experts, and with my own reservations. One, commenting from Switzerland, offered this chillingly prescient comment after my column was published: "Promoting the candidacy of Hillary Clinton, as the NYT seems to be doing, is equivalent to campaigning for a Republican win in 2016." That was some accurate crystal-ball gazing, considering that it was written in 2013.

In my columns, I documented the many strange chapters of this coverage. For instance, Chozick's feature story in the *Times* Sunday magazine about Clinton's wide sphere of influence was titled "Planet Hillary." The magazine's cover image of her face as a fleshy globe in space drew remarkable amounts of feedback, almost all negative. "This makes me crazy," NBC News's Andrea Mitchell, one of the most prominent women journalists in the country, was quoted in Talking Points Memo, expressing doubt that the *Times* Sunday magazine would ever portray a male political figure like this. And a reader, Kevin Egan, emailed me: "The now-viral image is hideously ugly, demeaning, sexist, and completely premature for an election almost three years away." *Times* editors, right up through Jill Abramson, who had approved the image in advance and called it "very apt," couldn't understand the fuss. Deputy magazine editor Lauren Kern argued that "it might not be flattering in physicality but it is in concept. She is an icon. It shows her power." From my point of view, it also showed that when it came to covering Hillary Clinton, *Times* journalists often took things too far.

The dustup over the Sunday magazine cover took place in January 2014, a relatively innocent time in the saga of Hillary Clinton and *The New York Times.* As the months rolled by, far more fraught issues arose. When the Breitbart contributor and right-wing partisan Peter Schweizer published his 2015 book *Clinton Cash: The Untold Story of How and Why Foreign Governments and Businesses Helped Make Bill and Hillary Rich,* the *Times* was there to cover it. Schweizer's credentials included heading the benign-sounding Government Accountability Institute. It's actually a right-wing outfit funded by and closely aligned with the family foundation of Robert Mercer, the hedge fund manager and eventual major Trump funder. Mercer was also a principal investor in Cambridge Analytica, the infamous British political consulting firm that misused the private data of Facebook users to benefit campaigns, including Trump's. This was Schweizer's crowd.

Regardless, the *Times* made an "exclusive" deal to pursue one of the story lines in his book, as did *The Washington Post* and Fox News, which raised the question of how exclusive such an arrangement really could be. But that wasn't the major concern. That was what one reader wrote to me: "I'm very unsettled that the *Times* is hyping a book by an extreme partisan." The arrangement, said another, "lends Schweizer's overall body of work a legitimacy it does not deserve." This is what I meant about the confounding paradox of the Clinton coverage. The sense of a "pre-anointed" candidate again was coupled with negative coverage that seemed to go beyond normal vetting and that seemed to lack perspective about what really deserved to be considered of great importance.

In her article about the publication of the book, Chozick's lead paragraph was less about the book's substance and more about its likely political ramifications, seen through the eyes of Clinton's critics and rivals. "The book does not hit shelves until May 5, but already the Republican Rand Paul has called its findings 'big news' that will 'shock people' and make voters 'question' the candidacy of Hillary Rodham Clinton," she wrote. There's nothing wrong, of course, with deeply investigating—"scrubbing," to use the newsroom lingo—a presidential candidate's background; in fact, it's crucially important to do so, part of the watchdog role of the press. Sometimes the leads for doing that kind of investigation come from "opposition research," the practice by political campaigns of digging up dirt on a political rival for the purpose of discrediting them. Journalists don't need to ignore this kind of negative information when they learn of it (often through a confidential tip from a campaign staffer); the question is whether reporters can dig into the facts and independently determine if a damaging accusation is not only true but also newsworthy.

When the *Times* got around to reporting on the substance of the one aspect of the Schweizer book they had decided to pursue (their "exclusive" area of interest), the paper published a front-page story, "Cash Flowed to Clinton Foundation amid Russian Uranium Deal." It hit hard, and was delicious catnip for right-wing politicos and their media allies, who quickly distorted and exaggerated it. Sean Hannity of Fox News was one of many who transformed this story into something much more diabolical. Though his position was unsupported by evidence, he implied that this proved that the U.S. secretary of state was corrupt and that she had risked national security for a quid pro quo deal to benefit herself through the Clinton Foundation. *This* was the Russia scandal to end all Russia scandals, if you believed Hannity. That kind of credulity is never a particularly good idea, though he and the Fox News network have millions of true believers and set the tone for right-wing coverage across the media. Clinton wanted to portray herself as the people's candidate, but this development gave her political opponents more ammunition to portray her as greedy, deceptive, and venal, as they often had in the past. Not for nothing did Hillary popularize the phrase "a vast, right-wing conspiracy" to describe the forces aligned against her and her husband that were constantly trying to drum up scandals to destroy them politically.

Was it wrong for the *Times* to publish that Clinton Foundation story? No, it was deeply reported and germane, but it may have been overplayed, with its importance overstated. It was consequential in hurting her politically because it deepened the portrayal that Republicans were eager to circulate. Again, the *Times*'s promise seemed to be: Yes, never fear, Hillary Clinton *will* be the next president but our readers will have an exaggerated sense of her flaws when she takes the oath of office.

The most damaging Clinton reporting was yet to come. By 2015 the presidential campaign was in full swing, and the public editor's email queue was always jammed with readers' complaints about the coverage. Bernie Sanders was being dismissed or even mocked by the *Times*. (To some extent, I agreed with this, and wrote about it.) Donald Trump's appalling past business dealings weren't getting much attention. And Clinton? As always, she stirred strong emotions of all kinds, and I constantly heard from readers about the coverage of her campaign and of her past.

In March, the *Times* reporter Michael Schmidt broke the story about her questionable email practices: the ill-advised use of a private computer server during her stint as secretary of state. In print, it appeared on the front page under the less than explosive headline "Clinton Used Personal Email at State Department." No big deal, you might think. But soon all hell broke loose, and it never stopped for the duration of the campaign. The press, and Clinton's many haters, became obsessed with the email scandal, if that's what it really was. Then, in July, Schmidt and Matt Apuzzo, another Washington bureau reporter, wrote a story—sourced anonymously—about the Justice Department opening a "criminal investigation" into Clinton regarding her email practices. Again, it got front-page treatment. But almost immediately Clinton's people got in touch with the *Times* and protested, calling its wording inaccurate. Quickly, and apparently in response to these complaints, the language in the story was changed; now the inquiry was called a "security referral," and the Justice Department inquiry was described in less personal terms. It was about the email practices, not about Clinton herself, as the story originally had stated. Two corrections were appended to the story; later, an editor's note was published, addressing how readers might have been confused by the changes and the conflicting information.

I wrote a blistering blog post and then a more tempered Sunday column about all of this, quoting executive editor Dean Baquet calling what had happened "a screw-up." My main takeaway was that the *Times* had been too hasty in publishing the story, especially since it was based on anonymous sources. "We got it wrong because our very good sources had it wrong," a deputy executive editor, Matt Purdy, told me at the time. This statement angered the readers who wrote in the comments section of my post, as well as many others angered by the paper's article, who said that this sounded all too familiar; it brought to mind the disastrous media coverage in the run-up to the Iraq War as the *Times,* and others, misleadingly reported the likely existence of weapons of mass destruction in Iraq and the close connections between Saddam Hussein and Al-Qaeda. This, too, was reporting that was based on some supposedly very good (anonymous) sources who got it wrong.

"You can't put stories like this back in the bottle," I wrote. Especially when published by the influential *New York Times,* "they ripple through the entire news system." The coverage throughout the media was out of proportion to the supposed crime. Looking back recently at all the coverage of Clinton's email practices, I was struck—and had to laugh out loud—at a sentence from a 2015 news story in the *Times.* It stated that public opinion polls showed voters' opinions of Clinton hadn't been swayed much by these revelations. That certainly was no longer true by the fall of 2016. Exploited endlessly by Trump and right-wing media, and heavily covered across the media spectrum, Hillary's email seemed to be all anyone could talk about, and it was the pretense used by Trump to get his crowds chanting "Lock her up!"

Then it got even worse with the arrival of the infamous Comey letter, which has become the topic of countless reconstructions and analyses. In late October, after discovering a trove of Clinton emails on a laptop belonging to Anthony Weiner, the estranged husband of Hillary's top aide, Huma Abedin, Comey reopened the FBI investigation into her email practices. Before that, the media's attention had moved on, at least somewhat. But with the public release of his letter to Congress on October 28, made with significant fanfare that went against FBI strictures, the email contretemps was front and center again. And just days before the presidential election.

The *Times* again overdid its coverage, making Comey's overreach even worse. Editors devoted the entire top of the print front page to this admittedly startling development and its potential ramifications: three articles and a photograph, all "above the fold" in print, and similarly dominant in digital form. One of the headlines, under the bylines of Amy Chozick and another politics reporter, Patrick Healy, read: "With 11 Days to Go, Trump Says Revelation 'Changes Everything.'" There must have been rejoicing in the GOP camp over that; they couldn't have framed it better themselves.

Later, two researchers would publish a story in *Columbia Journalism Review* finding that in just six days "the *New York Times* ran as many cover stories about Hillary Clinton's emails as they did about all the policy issues combined in the 69 days leading up to the election." Did it matter? Without a doubt. The statistics guru Nate Silver at fivethirtyeight.com analyzed the effects of the Comey letter (and, implicitly, the media coverage, led by the *Times*) in a post-election article: "It might have shifted the race by 3 or 4 percentage points toward Donald Trump, swinging Michigan, Pennsylvania, Wisconsin, and Florida to him, perhaps along with North Carolina and Arizona." Silver stopped short of saying it made all the difference, or stating that Clinton would have won if this hadn't happened. It certainly contributed, though—especially in combination with the breathless coverage of WikiLeaks's release of Clinton campaign chairman John Podesta's emails, and the relative lack of attention to Trump's own misdeeds. Of course, the right-wing media went overboard with all aspects of the Weiner/Abedin story, the development that set off the entire endgame of the campaign—a disastrous one for Hillary Clinton. The Murdoch-owned *New York Post,* whose editorial page endorsed Trump in the primary and which was a dependable supporter of his campaign on the news pages, splashed its story on the front page. A tawdry photo of Weiner in his underwear accompanied a just-as-tawdry headline that screamed, "HARD COPY: Huma Sent Weiner Classified Hillary Emails to Print Out."

Abedin herself knew how devastating this development was for Clinton's campaign. In an interview with CBS News about her 2021 memoir, *Both/And,* she looked back at the anger she felt toward her estranged husband, who ended up going to jail for sending lewd text messages to a minor—the offense that opened up the emails to the FBI. "This man Weiner was going to ruin me. And now he was going to jeopardize Hillary Clinton's chances of winning the presidency," Abedin wrote in her book, describing how she called him when the news broke. "'Anthony,' I said, wanting to shake him through the phone, 'if she loses this election, it will be because of you and me.'" She had a point.

High drama, indeed, and consequential, too. With less than two weeks to go before the election, it looked like the Clinton campaign was embroiled—again!—in the worst kind of sordid scandal, and that it was only escalating. Within a few days, the story had changed, and of course the media covered that, too. Comey decided to wrap up the FBI investigation again, after determining that there really was no problem here after all. Eventually the FBI had to issue a correction about his original statement that "hundreds and thousands" of emails were involved. It turned out to be only a few.

After the election, Comey was defensive about publicizing his reopening of the email investigation while simultaneously *not* disclosing the FBI's investigation of the Trump campaign's ties to Russia. "It makes me mildly nauseous to think that we might have had some kind of impact on the election," he told the Senate Judiciary Committee, though he stood by both decisions, saying they were consistent with FBI policy. Not everyone agreed. Many in Washington—not just Hillary supporters—thought Comey had gone too far, and portrayed him as a showboat. They criticized how he had been so public about reopening the investigation and had spoken so freely about Clinton, describing her and the State Department's handling of emails as "extremely careless," though he brought no charges and said no reasonable prosecutor would do so.

The *Times* had certainly treated the FBI's two investigations of the 2016 presidential candidates very differently. It shouted one from the rooftops, and on Trump and Russia the paper used its quiet inside voice, playing right into the Republican candidate's hands. With a little more than a week to go before the election, the *Times* published a story with the headline "Investigating Donald Trump, F.B.I. Sees No Clear Link to Russia." If anyone was concerned about Trump's ties to Vladimir Putin, their fears might be put to rest by that soothing headline, though the story itself was considerably more nuanced. Even that reporting, not very damning for Trump, appeared on an inside page of the paper, a far cry from the emails coverage splashed all over the front page, day after day. We now know, of course, that Russia *had* set out to interfere with the election, and did so very effectively.

David Brock—the conservative turned liberal activist, who founded Media Matters for America, the progressive media watchdog organization—went so far as to say that the *Times*'s Clinton coverage deserved "a special place in journalism hell." Brock was brutally critical. His incendiary 2015 book, titled *Killing the Messenger: The Right-Wing Plot to Derail Hillary and Hijack Your Government*, pointed directly at Carolyn Ryan, the *Times*'s senior politics editor, as a leading culprit. Relying on anonymous sources within the *Times* (which, as always, should give the reader plenty of pause), Brock wrote that "experienced journalists in the *Times* Washington bureau, I've been told, are appalled at Ryan's unprofessionalism on the Clinton beat. 'She has a hard-on for Hillary,' said one source in the *Times*. 'She wants that coonskin nailed to the wall.'"

Maybe some *Times* people did feel that way. From what I knew and observed, I don't believe that the paper, as an institution, was trying to get Trump elected or cause Clinton to lose. Nor do I believe that Ryan was playing out a personal vendetta. So why *did* this hugely influential news organization keep portraying Clinton so negatively and inflict so much damage? I come back to the same maddening answer: that it was because her presidency seemed inevitable, and they wanted to be tough on her before she became the leader of the free world. Often accused of liberal bias, the *Times* wanted to show clearly that this was not true, in coverage that implicitly shouted, "Look how tough we are on Hillary Clinton (your next president)." In addition, the news media, including *The New York Times,* loves to cover politics as a horse race. Since journalists across the board seemed to be convinced that Clinton would win handily, it made for a more exciting horse race if the favorite was loaded with extra weight to slow her down.

By the late spring of 2016, I had departed from the *Times* and begun a new job as media columnist at *The Washington Post.* So when the presidential campaign was in its last days, I was no longer in a position to demand that *Times* leadership tell me why they made the decisions they did. But my successor as public editor, Liz Spayd, commented more than once on the mild coverage of Russian interference in the election, such a contrast to the paper's Clinton coverage. The headline of one of Spayd's columns referred to a "muted alarm bell" on the relationship between Trump and Russia. She wrote, "This is an act of foreign interference in an American election on a scale we've never seen, yet on most days it has been the also-ran of media coverage, including at the *New York Times.*" Executive editor Dean Baquet bridled at the charge that the *Times* had held anything back. "We heard about the back-channel communications between the Russians and Trump," he told Spayd for her column. "We reported it, and found no evidence that it was true. We wrote everything we knew—and we wrote a lot. Anybody that thinks we sat on stuff is outrageous. It's just false."

All of this highly consequential coverage became—and still remains—a sore spot with a number of the *Times* journalists involved with those stories. My harsh criticism over the "criminal inquiry" story in 2015 struck some of them as unfair. Even after I left the paper for *The Washington Post,* I heard from more than one suggesting I revisit this in my new role as media columnist, recanting my earlier criticism. They pointed to a new *Times* story, published in 2017, in which the Justice Department essentially stated that the original reporting had been right all along, that there was no substantial difference between a "criminal investigation" and a "security referral" or a "security matter." That was, expressed in the reporters' own words in the story, "a distinction without a difference." After all, the argument went, the FBI is not the Federal Bureau of *Matters;* what it *does* is investigate crimes. It was no surprise to me that Comey, the centerpiece of that more recent story, would think so, and say so, since he or his top aides may well have been among the main sources for the since-corrected story.

What's more, if the "criminal inquiry" story was right to begin with, why had the *Times* seen fit to publish those two corrections, which remain to this day? If they were right to begin with, would they have to correct their own corrections? That never happened, although in addition to the appended corrections, the archived version of the story now begins with an italicized editor's note from 2018 (more than three years after the story was first published). That note directs readers to the "distinction without a difference" article from 2017 and to Comey's book, published the following year, for "additional light" on the subject. Well, maybe, but I'm not too sure any additional light was cast.

A reader coming fresh to that story today, with all of its piled-on baggage—two corrections and a years-later editor's note—would need a user's manual, a field guide, and a compass to figure out what had happened and what it all meant. I still think that the original language of "criminal inquiry," used in a front-page headline, was misguided, if not technically untrue. There are all kinds of ways to frame stories and all kinds of language choices to be made, particularly in headlines. Clinton later described the effect of that original "criminal investigation" story: "Now my campaign had to deal with questions about whether I was being measured for an orange jumpsuit." And I maintain that the chaotic way the changes were made to the story and headline, apparently under intense pressure from the Clinton campaign, was improper, confusing, and lacking in transparency. This flawed coverage, and its dire consequences, angered and alienated many *Times* readers, a fair number of whom haven't forgiven or forgotten what happened. In this way, too, it is similar to what happened with the Iraq run-up coverage; it has become a long-standing grievance. The difference is that there was no public mea culpa for the Clinton coverage, and perhaps not even an internal admission that anything was really wrong. I believe that many readers sense that self-satisfaction and are offended by it.

In her post-mortem book, Clinton expresses her resentment of the media coverage of her campaign, particularly the way it equalized her flaws and Trump's when they weren't close to equal. "If Trump ripped the shirt off someone at a rally, and a button fell off my jacket on the same day," she wrote, "the headline 'Trump and Clinton Experience Wardrobe Malfunctions, Campaigns in Turmoil' might feel equal to some but it wouldn't be balanced and it definitely wouldn't be fair."

As for the way she was treated in the nation's most influential newspaper, she had a few complaints there, too. The original email story, the one that set off all the endless coverage and near-hysteria in right-wing outlets, had real problems, she said. For example, it wasn't until the eighth paragraph that the story included the rather important fact that she was not the first government official, or secretary of state, to use a personal email account to conduct official business. She observed, accurately, that whatever the *Times* does tends to affect the entire media and politics ecosystem: "The facts didn't stop the hamster wheel of Washington scandal from spinning into rapid motion, as other media outlets sought to follow a story that must be important, because the *New York Times* had put it on the front page."

Clinton had become a tough press critic—and for good reason, since she'd had so much experience with being covered over many decades. Later, in one of my media columns for *The Washington Post,* I wrote about Clinton's book and asked Carolyn Ryan whether she and other editors had any regrets about the campaign coverage. I wanted to know whether any soul-searching had taken place. She was circumspect and acknowledged no blame. Reviewing political coverage, Ryan assured me, is "something we engage in all the time and have done so after this election." That internal review was focused on the use of public opinion polling, the need for reporters to get beyond New York and Washington, and how to dig more effectively into policy and issues. Though I pressed her, Ryan—frustratingly—wouldn't say whether those high-level newsroom conversations had taken up complaints about unfair coverage of the candidates, particularly from Clinton, or whether any reforms had been put in place.

Nor did the majority of the news media acknowledge they had gone too far with the infamous email story or that they had made serious errors with the campaign coverage in general, except to say that they needed to get out into "real America" more. (Not a bad idea, though it ended up producing what I called the Endless Diner Series, in which coastal reporters interviewed Trump voters in their hometown eateries, all competing to find the most "average" Americans and to learn that they hadn't changed their minds.)

In my view, the 2016 campaign coverage exposed the worst tendencies of the mainstream press: its addiction to sensation and the horse race, its propensity for overkill, and its profit-driven desire for clicks or TV ratings. The numbers told the story dramatically. The major broadcast TV networks gave only 32 minutes during 2016 to covering policy, but the email scandal got 100 minutes, according to a Tyndall Report study. This reflected a steady, sharp decline in policy coverage over the years. In 2008 the same networks gave a relatively generous 220 minutes to policy; in 2012 it was less, only 114 minutes. Meaningful coverage was dropping at a rapid pace. But CBS president David Rhodes shrugged off any wrongdoing when he was interviewed by former *Face the Nation* host Bob Schieffer: "There's always a blame-the-media phase of any campaign."

Cable news might have been worse. CNN's Jeff Zucker was pilloried at a post-election gathering at Harvard for how much free airtime his network gave to Trump's rallies and speeches while simultaneously going wild with coverage of the email scandal. Zucker responded by employing an absurd logical fallacy in his network's defense. "Half the people want to blame us for Trump, and half the people want to say that we're terrible to Trump," he said. "That's how I always think we're doing the right thing." It's one of journalism's most annoying and most self-satisfied axioms: If both sides are mad at us, we must be correct. That's often simply false, and certainly was when it came to 2016 campaign coverage. Much more on point was an analysis from the *Times*'s former Washington bureau chief, David Leonhardt, who criticized media organizations for how they handled a different email-related story: WikiLeaks's publication, late in the campaign, of thousands of emails stolen by Russian agents from Hillary Clinton's campaign. Leonhardt (at that point a *Times* opinion-side writer) wrote that the "over-hyped coverage of the hacked emails was the media's worst mistake in 2016." Fallout from the hacked emails did force the resignation of Debbie Wasserman Schultz from her post as Democratic National Committee chairwoman, because they showed DNC officials discussing how to undermine Bernie Sanders in the primary so that Clinton would be sure to win. Other than that, the hacked emails didn't produce much else of substance, and yet the gossipy revelations dominated many a news cycle and mixed with the *other* email scandal into a toxic, anti-Clinton stew. "I love WikiLeaks!" Trump crowed at a campaign rally, and he tweeted constantly about how the emails simply proved everything evil about "Crooked Hillary." Writing in *Esquire,* the astute politics blogger and former sportswriter Charles Pierce described the atmosphere around Hillary; he had seen it all before when her husband was president. "Any relatively commonplace political occurrence," Pierce wrote, "takes on mysterious dark energy when any Clinton is involved."

Whatever Hillary Clinton's complaints may have been about the *Times*'s coverage, she had to have been pleased to get their editorial endorsement, as she did at most newspapers in the United States. Only a handful of papers endorsed Trump. Many editorial boards issued warnings with what Jim Rutenberg, then the *Times* media columnist, described as a "collective sense of alarm" about what electing a dangerous demagogue, as *USA Today* put it, might portend. The *Times* editorial board—which functions separately from the newsroom, with its own staff and with many floors of physical separation—was almost effusive about Clinton. "Our endorsement," they wrote, "is rooted in respect for her intellect, experience, toughness and courage over a career of almost continuous public service, often as the first or only woman in the arena." The editorial made it clear that the *Times* endorsement was given on the candidate's own merits, not just in opposition to Trump, though the editorial described him as "the worst nominee put forward by a major party in modern American history." But, in my experience and observation, the editorial endorsements of newspapers—no matter how full-throated—rarely sway elections. However, relentless front-page political coverage can, especially when it's in the hugely influential *New York Times*. In this case, I believe it did.

There was a fitting coda. In the fall of 2019, almost three years into the Trump administration, Congress received a short report from the State Department that summarized its years-long investigation into Hillary's email practices while she was at the helm. Writing in *Vox*, Ian Millhiser described in shorthand the anticlimactic findings: "She shouldn't have done that. But it wasn't that big of a deal." The exculpatory study was received by the news media with a collective shrug. *The New York Times*—after all that—ran it on page A16.

6

Jill Abramson and Dean Baquet

The night before Jill Abramson's firing was announced, I sat across from her in a booth at a Lower Manhattan restaurant. Abramson knew what was about to happen the next day: She was about to be unceremoniously dumped as the first woman to hold the exalted position of executive editor of *The New York Times.* I, however, innocently eating my fancy pasta, had no idea what the next day would bring. Afterward, I found it remarkable that, knowing what she did, Abramson didn't cancel our dinner plans. Why would she spend her last evening in the most prestigious editorial post in American journalism by dining with me, someone who had been an annoying burr under her saddle? Why would she hang out with the public editor, the person whose job it was to critique *Times* journalism—and therefore, often, her decisions as its top editor—on behalf of the paper's readers? Jill and I weren't in the habit of socializing over meals, but she had recently turned sixty and I had suggested a dinner as a way to note that and to get past the tension that had developed in our relationship many months earlier.

The air had grown chilly between us ever since I started

to do research for a column that she vehemently objected to. I wanted to investigate how, roughly ten years earlier, *The New York Times* had withheld an important story—for thirteen long months—in deference to national security objections from the George W. Bush administration. Jill wasn't the top editor back then, but she was a ranking newsroom leader, high up in the Washington bureau, who was involved with the story. That withheld story, about the way the U.S. government was secretly wiretapping its own citizens, was a crucial early look at the American surveillance state that had developed after 9/11; after it was finally published, it won a Pulitzer Prize. It might never have been published at all if one of its authors, the prominent investigative reporter James Risen, hadn't held a metaphorical gun to his editors' heads by declaring that he would soon be publishing his reporting in his book *State of War.*

A look back was germane because of something that had happened more recently: The whistleblower Edward Snowden, a former National Security Agency contractor, had not brought his bombshell story, about a cache of inside information regarding government surveillance, to the *Times.* As he told a journalist, those who put themselves in danger to leak information to the press "must have absolute confidence that the journalists they go to will report on that information rather than bury it." He lacked that confidence in the *Times,* based on what had happened with the infamous thirteen-month delay, so he ultimately cooperated with *The Guardian* and *The Washington Post,* a big blow to the *Times.*

Learning of my intentions, Abramson summoned me and bluntly told me she didn't think it was in my job description to go digging around in the past, taking up things that had happened a full decade before I began my stint as public editor. (I had been sitting in Risen's backyard in suburban Washington, interviewing him for the column, when one of Abramson's deputies left me an urgent-sounding message to see her soon and gave me a hint of why.) I was stunned. After all, I didn't report to her, even indirectly.

To her mind, such a column simply wasn't fair game. My job, she insisted, was to critique *Times* journalism in the present tense and to deal with the concerns of readers as they arose in real time. This, she believed, was out of bounds. She told me that she also felt protective of her predecessor as top editor, Bill Keller, whose managing editor she eventually became; it was Keller who had decided to withhold the story, on the strong advice of then-Washington bureau chief Philip Taubman. For many reasons, Jill simply didn't want to dredge up that whole episode again.

In fact, she warned me that if I insisted on writing the piece, she might take an extreme step: she'd consider cutting off communication with me altogether. We had some tough words about it, a conversation that was gut-wrenching for me, by far the most upsetting encounter I had had at the *Times* so far. I still cringe to remember that while sitting in her spacious corner office—the pinnacle of editorial power in American media—I mortified myself by starting to cry as she made her strong objections known. (Despite the axiom "there's no crying in newsrooms," I've managed to shed embarrassing tears in most of the places I've worked, from the *Niagara Gazette* to *The New York Times*.) Still, my courage didn't fail me about what really mattered. I knew what I had to do: Go ahead with the column and let the chips fall where they may. I knew Abramson wouldn't go so far as to order it killed. That would be beyond the pale, especially since a number of staffers were already aware it was in the works, which I pointed out to her. There seemed to be no other choice but to continue, *especially* after she told me not to. As public editor, I was supposed to be completely independent; it was a central tenet of the job description.

As it turned out, nothing terrible happened to me, to Jill, or to Bill Keller as a result of the column. I reported it as rigorously and fairly as I could, even interviewing Michael V. Hayden, the former CIA director and former director of the NSA, and, of course, all the key *Times* figures, including the since-retired Taubman. Hayden made a little news for me by stating unequivocally that the government never would have attempted to keep the *Times* from publishing had editors chosen to go ahead: "Prior restraint was never in the cards."

I interviewed Keller, by then a columnist, who was forthcoming about why he made the decision to hold back the story on national security grounds. He talked about the atmosphere in the country after 9/11, saying that those kinds of concerns loomed large. "Three years after 9/11, we, as a country, were still under the influence of that trauma, and we, as a newspaper, were not immune," Keller said as we sat in his office several floors above the newsroom he had run. "It was not a kind of patriotic rapture. It was an acute sense that the world was a dangerous place." He advised me against judging something in hindsight without understanding the moment in which it occurred. I took his point, but I still thought it had been the wrong move, one far too deferential to the government. The delay meant that publication came *after* George W. Bush's reelection, not when it might have swayed some voters. Keller expressed doubt about whether publication would have made much of a difference politically: "It's become an unexamined article of faith" on the left, he said, that publication in the fall of 2004 might have given John Kerry the presidency.

My column was read appreciatively, perhaps adding something worthy to the historical record, but it certainly never went viral. After all that drama, its publication was anticlimactic and it was time to move on to other, more current subjects. Nevertheless, I look back on that column, "Lessons in a Surveillance Drama Redux," as one of the best pieces I did; it raises important questions and holds up well. I'm glad I had the guts to go forward with it over the internal resistance, despite my own trepidation.

The incident had left Jill and me on awkward terms (at least *I* thought so) for quite a while, and I hoped to change that. After all, it would be prudent to keep cordial relations with the executive editor, if possible, and not to let a permanent rift develop. What's more, I admired Jill in so many ways: her high intelligence, the journalism she had fostered, her strength of character, the book about Supreme Court justice Clarence Thomas she had written with *The New Yorker*'s Jane Mayer—and certainly her pioneering role at the *Times,* which was similar to my breakthrough appointment in Buffalo, though on a much larger stage. I was no fangirl, but I appreciated spending time in this storied newsroom, run for the first time by a woman. So I had suggested we get together for dinner, and she suggested the restaurant, a Soho favorite of hers: Raoul's. It seemed like a pleasant enough idea for a weeknight outing. Especially since I didn't know that the hammer was about to come down.

The next morning, the *Times* publisher—Arthur Sulzberger, Jr.—stopped by my office, asking if I was planning to be in the newsroom later. There would be an all-hands meeting, and he thought I would want to attend, even though I wasn't really a member of the staff in the usual sense. Something in his demeanor made me think this had some momentous consequence. My reporter's antennae went up. What's it all about? I asked him. He wouldn't say. I was so curious that, while he was standing in my office that Wednesday morning, I took a stab at it to see how he would react. Jill is stepping down, I guessed, and you're installing Dean Baquet as editor. Sulzberger looked stunned, and asked who had told me that. No one, I said, which was the truth. But something about Abramson's demeanor and remarks at dinner the night before, combined with a recent conversation I had had with *Times* media columnist David Carr about the contentious relationship between publisher and editor, gave me a flash of intuition. As it turned out, a few hours later, there would be no gentle "stepping down" from her lofty post. No pretense about wanting to explore other career options (as if there could be other career options for the top editor of *The New York Times*). Abramson—the first woman to run the *Times* newsroom—had been summarily fired after less than three years on the job. This was legitimately shocking.

But why was she fired? That's what everyone wanted to know. Was it, as some of her women supporters believed, that she was the victim of sexism—seen as "too pushy," when a man exhibiting the same behavior would have been seen as forceful and, at most, a tough, demanding boss? People started making comparisons to Howell Raines, another fired *Times* editor, but one who had been treated with more deference—he was given the chance to say goodbye to the staff, for one thing—and who had had a full-fledged journalism scandal happen on his watch: the Jayson Blair fabrication and plagiarism mess.

Was Abramson a poor administrator, prone to management mistakes, like the way she had moved to hire a second managing editor without getting buy-in from Baquet, the one already doing that second-in-command job? Or was something else going on—something that had a lot to do with the hierarchical structure of the *Times,* still run by the Sulzberger dynasty, and a lot to do with a vision for the future of the institution? Not long before Abramson's firing, the young man who would soon become publisher—Arthur Gregg Sulzberger, known as A.G.—had been the driving force behind a document that had become known informally as the Innovation Report. (In fact, Abramson herself helped choose A.G., who then was barely into his thirties, for that leading role.) After she was fired, a summary of the report was leaked to the news media, and eventually the full report was published. Meant to assess the *Times*'s ability to stay on top of evolving technology and tastes, the gist of the report was that the newsroom wasn't moving nearly quickly enough, or fully enough, into the digital age. *Print was over.* Discussions of which seven stories should appear on the next morning's front page shouldn't be the focal point of every day. Huge, seismic change was taking place in the media business, and the *Times* needed to be leading the way. Writing about it in Harvard's Nieman Lab, Joshua Benton commented on how raw its self-criticism was: "You can sense the frayed nerves and the frustration at a newsroom that is, for all its digital successes, still in many ways oriented toward an old model."

Inside the *Times,* the report was a huge topic of conversation and, mostly, agreement: We needed to break through the barriers and move forward more boldly. "The *New York Times* is winning at journalism," the report began. "At the same time, we are falling behind in a second critical area: the art and science of getting our journalism to readers. . . . We haven't done enough to crack that code in the digital era." The report said that the two major competitors, *The Washington Post* and *The Wall Street Journal,* were further along; it also mentioned admiringly the digital progress of other news organizations like *Vox, USA Today,* and *The Guardian.* And it said that, frequently, more traffic to *Times* stories was coming from news aggregators like Flipboard than from the *Times* itself. Here was a particularly devastating set of findings: "Over the last year, the *Times* has watched readership fall significantly. Not only is the audience on our website shrinking but our audience on our smartphone apps has dipped, an extremely worrying sign on a growing platform."

Abramson, who justifiably prided herself on encouraging digital projects such as the groundbreaking "Snow Fall," with its arresting graphic treatment of a deadly avalanche, objected to the idea that she wasn't pushing hard enough into the digital world. She and Baquet jointly issued a memo that said they approved of the report's major recommendations. There was some doubt, though, about whether she fully embraced them. Was she willing to work closely and cooperatively with the business side of the company, rather than trying to preserve the firm, traditional separation between the newsroom and the bean counters? Not enough, apparently, for the younger Sulzberger and those he trusted most. True, his father was still in charge, but probably not for long; A.G.'s opinion mattered tremendously.

And then there was the Dean Baquet factor. At the newsroom meeting where Abramson's firing was announced to a stunned staff, Sulzberger also announced, with a celebratory air, that Abramson's second-in-command would become the paper's first Black executive editor. Had Baquet given Sulzberger something of an ultimatum, along the lines of "Do something about Jill or I'll leave the *Times*"? Maybe, some speculated, it was even stronger: "It's her or me. Pick." Baquet denied in an NPR interview that he ever gave such an ultimatum to Sulzberger, though he said he did make it clear to the publisher that he was unhappy. I asked Baquet about it myself shortly after his ascent to executive editor, and he answered in words that acknowledged the Roman Catholic upbringing that we shared: "I've examined my conscience on this, and it's clear." (I didn't offer to help him examine it more closely.)

Given Abramson's various management missteps, both in managing up to her powerful boss and down to her staff—many of whom had become disillusioned with her sometimes brusque management style while still respecting her as a journalist—the choice apparently seemed fairly obvious to Sulzberger. He had already overseen the departure of a high-ranking Black editor, Gerald Boyd, who had been Howell Raines's managing editor and who had had a role in enabling Jayson Blair's wrongdoing, as he'd mentored the young Black reporter. In other words, it would look very bad to have Baquet leave the *Times*, especially if he did so unhappily.

Baquet's personality was very different from Abramson's, though they had some qualities in common. Like Jill, Dean was an accomplished and respected journalist; his investigative reporting for the *Chicago Tribune* back in the 1980s had earned him a Pulitzer Prize, and, like Abramson, he had run the *Times*'s Washington bureau. What's more, the New Orleans native was gregarious, always ready with a teasing joke or a just-invented nickname. The weather around Dean was perpetually sunny. Except, of course, when his notorious temper flared; in 2013, after a disagreement with Abramson, his boss, he slammed his hand against a wall in the newsroom and left the building for the rest of the day. Later, in an interview with Politico, Baquet admitted he hadn't behaved well: "I feel bad about that. The newsroom doesn't need to see one of its leaders have a tantrum." But the main thrust of the article in Politico depicted not Baquet but Abramson in the most negative light, anonymously quoting critics in the newsroom who called her impossible to deal with and said she frequently blew up at editors in meetings. Somehow, Baquet's temper tantrum came off as a poor reflection on *her.*

Another time, Baquet shot back at one of his critics, a journalism professor, in a Facebook exchange, calling him an "asshole." The professor, Marc Cooper, had slammed Baquet—charging "absolute cowardice"—for not publishing controversial cartoons from the French satirical magazine *Charlie Hebdo,* where twelve people had died after an attack by Islamic terrorists in early 2015. The Baquet-Cooper dustup turned into a media-news story for days. I happened to be in Baquet's office interviewing him the day that the exchange came to light. An editor popped her head in, carrying her open laptop, to warn Baquet with considerable alarm that his Facebook page had apparently been hacked; she had seen the nasty name-calling, and of course assumed that the executive editor of *The New York Times* would never utter such a word on social media. "Oh, yeah, I wrote that," Baquet told her, laughing; she nodded, looking stunned, and quietly backed out of his office. He could get away with almost anything because of his charm and because he had the complete backing of the *Times* publisher, who, after all, couldn't fire two executive editors in a row, or three in only fifteen years, counting

Raines. He also clearly enjoyed Baquet's company and admired his journalism.

Sulzberger's pride in naming the first woman executive editor had been real, but from his point of view it hadn't paid off in the long run. Now, though, he could brag about another groundbreaking "first" because of Baquet's race. And he clearly felt much more comfortable with the choice, one that would last into the next decade until Baquet reached retirement age. (At the *Times*, high-ranking editors traditionally step down at the end of their sixty-fifth year of age.) Abramson, for her part, endured after the crisis. After all, she had been through worse, having survived a terrible pedestrian accident: She was hit by a delivery truck in Manhattan in 2007 and, as a result, had been hospitalized for a long period as she recovered. After leaving the *Times*, she began teaching narrative writing at her alma mater, Harvard, and wrote a book about journalism in the digital age.

Although Jill and I had had some harsh disagreements, I was disturbed to see her unseated so abruptly as top editor. In retrospect, I've come to think that her response to the Innovation Report—something short of an unquestioning embrace—was the biggest factor. Abramson felt strongly about preserving the traditional strict separation between the newsroom and the business side of the paper. The idea that journalists and marketing or advertising people should be working closely together on projects didn't sit well with her. The report advocated for that wall coming down, although it acknowledged the need to preserve editorial independence. Journalism was changing fast, and the *Times* had no intention of being left behind. In her book *Merchants of Truth,* Abramson addresses in detail and with considerable honesty what brought about her firing. Although that section was not a major part of her book and was a bit off its main theme, *New York* magazine published it as an excerpt in early 2019, anticipating correctly the great interest of many who had wondered what on earth could have been behind her firing.

The Innovation Report was, Abramson wrote, "an epic defeat" for her and a terribly disappointing one because she had been "so determined and worked so hard to be the transitional editor who would succeed in making the newsroom digital-first without causing a cultural meltdown or letting the best traditions die, like protecting the news from being colored by the crass commercialism I saw on news sites across the internet." She described the report as "a call to arms" for something that *Times* CEO Mark Thompson wanted desperately: more collaboration between the news and business sides.

But Abramson also carefully and candidly went through the other factors: She had been clumsy in handling an important personnel decision, as she moved to hire a second managing editor without communicating with the one she already had. That, understandably, put Baquet's nose out of joint, since he was Abramson's second-in-command. She also pointed to her efforts to be paid as much as her predecessors in the editor's role. She both admitted her own weaknesses and made it clear she had been treated poorly. She also wrote that, as editor, she had felt "lonely and depressed" at work, something I found poignant because I always perceived her as confident to the point of being high-handed. During the end game of her tenure, her integrity shone through; she refused to sign off on a *Times* press release that said she was voluntarily resigning. Abramson's attitude was that she'd always been a truth-teller and wasn't about to change that now. Her attitude, in essence: I'm getting fired, so let's call it what it is.

As all of this unfolded in 2014, I wrote several blog posts about what was happening, and tried to explore the reasons. I'm not proud of those pieces; I wasn't able to shed much light, and my reporting didn't yield much of value. *The New Yorker*'s Ken Auletta did much better, as did the *Times*'s own David Carr. But I did try to evaluate Abramson's performance as executive editor. While acknowledging her management missteps, I gave her credit for a tenure that had been free of scandal; she had "kept the paper straight," which was one of her stated aims. She moved the journalism forward into the digital realm. She defended press rights and stood up for her reporters, most notably with the tough reporting on the Chinese government, which brought howls and threats from its subjects. And during her brief reign, the paper won eight Pulitzer Prizes. What's more, I wrote, "she wore her feminism on her sleeve in just the right way—not with overplaying stories about women's issues, but with the determined promotion of qualified women into top roles." She had moved several women into editorial positions that would position them to be at the very top of the *Times* newsroom when the next changing of the guard came.

I'd go so far as to say elite journalism was never the same. It's impossible to overstate, for one thing, the importance of having a woman in the top position in the *Times* newsroom, something that had never happened before and that, when she was named, had still not happened at *The Washington Post* or many other major news organizations. A decade later, that would change dramatically. Abramson brought other women up along with her, not only on the masthead but on major beats, with an eye to increasing women's bylines on the front page. From all I've heard, she was influential in my appointment as public editor, too. Although it was the publisher, not the editor, who had the final call, she had told Sulzberger that hiring a fifth white male public editor would be a bad look and a missed opportunity. Accordingly, the two finalists for the job were both women.

I owe her a debt of gratitude, and we've remained on good terms, though we're very different people. Abramson and I have a mutual friend: David Shribman, a former *Times* man who had a stint at *The Buffalo News* before I worked there and went on to an outstanding career. At one point, while trying to work through a period of tension with Abramson, I had talked to him, and to his wife, Cindy Skrzycki of *The Washington Post*. David, droll and incisive as always, characterized the difference between his two friends, and a possible reason for occasional misunderstanding. "Jill is an uptown girl," Shribman said. "You're not." I didn't like the sound of that; I thought it made her sound urbane and sophisticated and me like a rube. But when I mentioned Shribman's words to my daughter, then in college at New York University, she offered a perspective that changed the way I looked at it (a specialty of hers): "I wouldn't say that's such a bad thing." Perhaps there was a benefit to not being part of the coastal elite. Grace's view was wise, I realized, especially since I did see myself in that

Nick Carraway role: the midwesterner who comes east and, because he is an outsider, sees the world of Gatsby with a fresh perspective.

My public editor stint was almost evenly split between Jill's and Dean's editorships. My role was such that I had plenty of contact with both of them. As issues would arise that I thought deserved my attention, I would sometimes get in touch with section editors or, less frequently, with the reporters. Sometimes that would be enough, as was the case with the Yvonne Brill obituary controversy, in which I interviewed the writer and the obituaries editor. At other times, I would get a response from the standards editor, Phil Corbett, particularly on issues about possible ethics violations or about language use (for example, whether the *Times* should keep using the phrase "illegal immigrant").

However, there were some instances when only a response from the executive editor would be sufficient. Generally, once I decided to pursue an issue (there were always plenty to choose from and I could never get to them all), I emailed the editor I wanted a response from; almost always I got their attention quickly. At that point, they either responded by email or suggested I stop into their office to see them. They rarely came to see me. And, with few exceptions, any interaction with ranking *Times* editors was understood to be on the record; if it wasn't, there had to be a mutually agreed-upon understanding about that. Doing it any other way would have made me a part of the editorial team, which I never wanted to be. I had to keep some professional distance, and one way of doing that was to consider myself a reporter at all times and to behave like one.

As with Abramson, I had some rough moments with Baquet as well, though overall I found him more approachable. Sometimes, though, he was impulsive and temperamental. In one instance, he misread an email I had sent him about what I intended to say in a post, as I asked for his response. When he read my post online after publication a few hours later, he fired off an email to me, suggesting that I had misled him about the point of view I intended to take. He actually used the word "sleazy" to describe what he thought I had done. I was shocked and pushed back hard: For one thing, I told him, you're wrong on the facts; check my original email. For another, you cannot use that word with me. When he realized that he had misunderstood me, and that in any case his adjective was out of line, he apologized profusely and immediately.

With one of his deputies in tow, he soon showed up in my office to make his apology in person. As Baquet stood in the doorway, he uttered one of the strangest (and funniest) phrases I'd ever heard: "Can you hug the public editor?" I laughed, held up one hand with palm outward, and said, "No, thanks." I accepted his apology and we moved on.

At the drama-rich *Times*—no matter who was in charge—there was always another dustup, another controversy, to contend with. Baquet would suffer his share of these, including some of his own making; a number of these happened after I had moved on from the *Times*. He mishandled the departure from the paper (a resignation under pressure) of the revered science writer Donald McNeil, who had uttered a racial slur while on an educational trip with high school students. McNeil defended himself by saying that he used the "*n*-word" only because he was in a conversation about whether a student who had used the word elsewhere should have been suspended from school; in my view, his saying the word at all showed terrible judgment. But the punishment—being pushed out of the *Times* after a forty-year career, following internal protests by his colleagues—seemed too severe.

Baquet was the one who made the call about how to display (or, I believe, vastly overplay) the consequential story of FBI director James Comey's reopening of the investigation into Hillary Clinton's email practices less than two weeks before the 2016 presidential election. It was on his watch, too, that the *Times* had to retract the core of its celebrated *Caliphate* podcast, because its main source had fabricated his story, and return the Peabody Award it had won. When these later controversies and others were exploding and the critics were in attack mode on Twitter (often for good reason), I would issue my standard tweet: "It's another good day not to be the NYT public editor."

For anyone in the top editor's position, some missteps are inevitable. At the *Times*, they tend to be very public and can get ugly fast. But, unlike Abramson, Baquet usually got the benefit of the doubt internally. Nothing stuck. That may have been the result of his sunny personality, or his understanding of how to handle the boss (whether the older or the younger Sulzberger), or his greater popularity with the staff. Whether through luck or skill, talent or timing, he has survived—and thrived.

As Baquet turned sixty-five in September 2021, the question of who would succeed him as executive editor became the topic of even more heated speculation than usual. Reading the tea leaves about succession is a never-ending obsession at the *Times* and in the broader media world. Joseph Kahn, who held the second-in-command role of managing editor and is a former China correspondent for the *Times*, was the obvious choice, and indeed did get the all-important nod in late April of the following year. I was glad to see it. Among all the senior editors I dealt with, Kahn showed some of the most consistent good judgment; he struck me as not only particularly intelligent but also open to criticism. Although his own background is eastern seaboard Brahmin (he grew up in Boston and was president of the *Harvard Crimson*), he clearly has a strong feeling for the less fortunate, winning a Robert F. Kennedy Journalism Award for reporting on labor conditions in China's export factories and a Pulitzer Prize, shared with Jim Yardley, for stories on the often-unfair justice system in China.

When I brought divisive issues to him in his role supervising the international news coverage, I found Kahn to be accessible, nonimpulsive, and nondefensive. He was particularly thoughtful when I decided to address the extremely thorny subject of the paper's coverage of Israel and Palestine, and made some suggestions in my column for improving that coverage. (The topic is so fraught, such an obvious no-win, that my first line was "This is the column I never wanted to write.") Kahn understood the role of the public editor, including the notion that I represented readers and that it might be wise to listen to them sometimes. I doubt, though, that he would ever advocate for reinstating the position, a decision that would be made by the publisher, not the editor; *nobody* wants that trouble. It will be surprising to me if he doesn't turn out to be an excellent executive editor who will bring less drama than some of his predecessors. I wrote in a *Post* column shortly after he was named that Kahn's success (or lack thereof) will depend on how he directs politics and government coverage at this crucial moment when American democracy is on the brink. My pressing questions: "Will the paper's coverage forthrightly identify the problems posed by a radicalized Republican Party that is increasingly dedicated to lies, bad-faith attacks and the destruction of democratic norms, or will it try to treat today's politics as simply the result of bipartisan 'polarization'? Will it try to cut the situation straight down the middle as if we were still in the old days—an era that no longer exists?" Ever-influential, the *Times* needs to show strong leadership, and, of course, that comes directly from the top.

Naturally, I would love to see another woman or person of color run the *Times* newsroom someday; there are a number of such editors a bit further down in the editorial hierarchy, and Kahn quickly named Marc Lacey, who is Black, and Carolyn Ryan as his top deputies. With their appointments, a new round of speculation—will one of them succeed Kahn?—began even before Baquet stepped down. Thankfully, a lot has changed since the days, not so long ago, of all-white, all-male newsroom leadership. And still more change is necessary.

7

Small Victories

After reading a column of mine that warned about the news media's role in the perilous state of American democracy, my sister-in-law Catherine texted me to ask if I ever felt like Cassandra: the Trojan princess in Greek mythology who was cursed to warn, accurately, of future disasters but who was never believed. "More like Sisyphus," I shot back, without having to give it any thought. I was referring, of course, to another figure from Greek myth, the one who was forced as a punishment to roll a massive boulder up a mountain only to have it roll down again, at which point he would start over again. For all eternity.

I often felt like Sisyphus during my stint as *New York Times* public editor. After hearing complaints from readers or through my own observation, I would identify repeated practices that seemed harmful to the paper's effectiveness, integrity, or credibility, and I would write about them. Occasionally I could get top editors to agree that there *might* be a problem or even that there had been a bad mistake. At other times, they would decline to acknowledge that something had gone wrong, though it clearly had. And then, either way, whatever it was would happen again and again.

For example, *Times* journalists sometimes failed to give due credit to smaller news organizations (and, remember, every other news organization was smaller, comparatively) that had broken a story first. In general, they were more conscientious about this with major publications like *The Washington Post* or *The Wall Street Journal,* and worse with academic publications, local or foreign papers, or small start-ups. This was maddening for editors and reporters elsewhere who felt as though their hard, often underfunded work had been inadequately acknowledged by the powerful *Times;* in many cases, all they really wanted was a phrase of attribution ("the *Belarusian Journal of Obscure Disorders* wrote about this last August"), or even just a hyperlink to their story. But too often that didn't happen, and I would hear back from *Times* reporters or editors, asserting wide-eyed innocence: They had never even *seen* that earlier work. Sometimes, I'm sure, this was true. And sometimes such assertions were a little hard to believe.

It certainly could be frustrating to feel I was doing no good while enduring the hassles of the job. By early 2015, with two and a half years under my belt, the strain was getting to me. One critic of my work had accused me of writing "pious sermonettes"—in other words, of having the nerve to point out faults and to do so in what he considered a holier-than-thou tone. (I don't think this was generally true; I tried to avoid lecturing.) Another one disparagingly called me—as if this were some kind of a wounding insult—"a truth vigilante." That was the kind of vicious putdown I could happily accept. One of my journal entries from this period reads like a cri de coeur: "I don't know how much more of this gig I can take." But then there would be a good day or two, and I would bounce back, ready for more and, on balance, glad to be doing this strange job to the best of my ability. Piously or not.

One of the worst repeating problems, as I've noted, was the *Times*'s overuse of unnamed sources, also known as "confidential sources" or "anonymous sources." There were instances when the reliance on that kind of sourcing created real problems, but—in keeping with the Sisyphus syndrome—my pointing this out had had little effect. The policy of using unnamed sources only as a "last resort," according to one *Times* editorial dictum, was widely ignored. Every day's edition of the *Times* seemed to have information attributed to "a U.S. official" or "a White House official." Sometimes even frothy feature stories featured quotations from someone who couldn't speak on the record for one obscure reason or another.

I had been at the *Times* for more than three years when this problem came to a head in late 2015 with the tragic San Bernardino massacre. It was the deadliest mass shooting since a gunman had slaughtered twenty schoolchildren and six adults three years earlier at Connecticut's Sandy Hook Elementary School. In San Bernardino, a married couple targeted a county-run training event and holiday party in a terror attack that killed fourteen people and seriously injured many more. Terrible in itself, but then came a serious *Times* reporting error. A front-page article stated that the U.S. government had missed something that should have been an obvious red flag, something that could even have prevented the attack by refusing to allow the perpetrators to enter the United States. The red flag, according to the story, was the jihadist social media activity by one of the San Bernardino killers. The article began:

> Tashfeen Malik, who with her husband carried out the massacre in San Bernardino, Calif., passed three background checks by American immigration officials as she moved to the United States from Pakistan. None uncovered what Ms. Malik had made little effort to hide—that she talked openly on social media about her views on violent jihad. She said she supported it. And she said she wanted to be a part of it.

It was appalling—or so it seemed—that the American national security and immigration apparatus had missed such a thing. The problem, though, was that the key element of the article was wrong. Malik had not "talked openly" on social media about her support of violent jihad. She had written emails; she had posted on a dating site; she had written private messages. But that wasn't the way it was depicted on the Sunday front page of the *Times*, under a headline reading "Visa Screening Missed an Attacker's Zealotry on Social Media." As usual, the *Times*'s reporting got picked up everywhere. And the reaction soon turned political. Ted Cruz, the Texas senator who hoped to get the Republican nomination for president, began trumpeting the failures of the Obama administration, charging it with putting political correctness—extended to terrorists—above safety and national security. At a Republican presidential primary debate in Las Vegas, he used that story for some performative rage against Democrats: The administration "didn't monitor the Facebook posting of the female San Bernardino terrorist because the Obama [Department of Homeland Security] thought it would be inappropriate. She made a public call to jihad and they didn't target it." Of course, Malik had *not* made a public call to jihad, though the *Times* reported that she had.

I took this on in a column, after the truth came out and the story was corrected. Even the usually *Times*-friendly James Comey had to admit the news report was "a garble," which was an understatement since its major premise was simply wrong. I came down hard and called for "systemic change." The article's publication, I wrote, "involved a failure of sufficient skepticism at every level of the reporting and editing process—especially since the story in question relied on anonymous government sources, as too many *Times* articles do." In this case, top editors were in agreement with me, though they defended the reporters for all the good work they had done in the past, pointing out that one of them had won a Pulitzer Prize. How did this happen? The explanation was embarrassing. The story's sources, Dean Baquet told me, didn't understand the difference between public posts on social media and direct messages that are not public. But, I pressed, if these messages were believed to be public, why hadn't *Times* reporters insisted on seeing them? That seemed like due diligence, especially for a story this important. Baquet responded that insisting on seeing the posts would have been unrealistic given the time pressures of a deadline, but he agreed that a problem had been exposed.

"This was a really big mistake," Baquet told me, "and more than anything since I've become editor, it does make me think we need to do something about how we handle anonymous sources." He called it "a system failure that we have to fix." However, he said, it would not be realistic or advisable to ban anonymous sources entirely. I didn't disagree with that. I knew that giving sources the cover of anonymity is sometimes the only way to get important information to the public.

To his credit, Baquet took action. In mid-March 2016—about twelve weeks after the San Bernardino debacle, and not long before I wrapped up my public editor stint—the *Times* rolled out a new policy on handling anonymous sources. Its major tenet required that one of three top editors (including Baquet) must review and sign off on articles that depend primarily on information from unnamed sources. This would particularly concern those stories that "hinge on a central fact" from such a source, deputy executive editor Matt Purdy told me. That had been the case with the San Bernardino story. I wrote about the new policy, quoting Purdy calling those stories potential "journalistic I.E.D.s"—in other words, they were bombs that could explode unexpectedly and damage the *Times* and its credibility. Given their danger, he had told me, they required special oversight, and a process that may result in slowing down before publication. *Times* editors were clear in saying that they had been working on some new rules for a while; they didn't credit me with making it happen. And that was fine with me; I didn't need a citation with a gold seal from Arthur Sulzberger to hang on my wall. But I do believe I played a role.

The reform of the policy on the use of anonymous sources felt like something of a bookend to the *Times*'s changed policy on "quote approval" that I had pushed hard for at the beginning of my time as public editor back in 2012. In that case, reporters were instructed to stop allowing sources and their spokespeople to review, in writing, quotations from a background interview. It had become the norm for reporters, not just at the *Times,* to interview a newsmaker "on background," meaning not for direct quotation. Then reporters would email quotes they wanted to use in their stories to the newsmaker's spokesperson or to the sources themselves. And the spokesperson, or source, would either approve the quotes or decline them—or, frequently, change them to make them more acceptable in some way. That meant that, in many cases, direct quotes used in news stories were never actually uttered in an interview. Quote approval gave sources—both in government and in business—far too much control over what the *Times* would publish. Even after the policy was changed, I have no doubt that the practice of quote approval continued at the *Times* to some extent, but at least reporters were able to push back on their sources by saying there was a newsroom policy against it. The Associated Press banned quote approval, too. As an AP spokesman put it, their journalists don't allow sources to say, in effect, "I want those three sentences you want to use sent over to me to be put through my rinse cycle." The *Times*'s own media columnist, David Carr, had written about the general practice by journalists, though he didn't take up his own employer's policy specifically: "Inch by inch, story by story, deal by deal, we are giving away our right to ask a simple question and expect a simple answer. It may seem obvious but it is still worth stating: The first draft of history should not be rewritten by the people who make it." Amen.

I applied pressure by urging that the *Times* ban the practice. My push to do so was magnified by articles in other publications about my effort. I was gratified to have had some kind of role in getting quote approval banned—though, just as with the reform measures on anonymous sources, *Times* editors were clear that they didn't do this because of me. It had been in the works before I came along. I just gave it a big public shove in the right direction.

Both reforms—quote approval and anonymous sources—were important. But the change on anonymous sources meant more to me. As I had learned through all my correspondence with *Times* readers over more than three years, they hadn't forgotten the damage wrought by the use of unnamed sources in the prelude to the disastrous Iraq War. Some of them, no doubt, had watched the powerful PBS program in 2007, "Buying the War: How Big Media Failed Us," in which the great Bill Moyers made it nauseatingly clear how the American press, again led by *The New York Times,* got on board with the patriotic fervor sweeping the nation after 9/11. It detailed how little skepticism mainstream journalists demonstrated regarding the claims being made by the George W. Bush administration about the supposed close connections between

Saddam Hussein and the terrorist group Al-Qaeda, which had carried out the 9/11 attacks, and about Saddam's supposed development of chemical, biological, and nuclear weapons. "There was a real sense that you don't get that critical of a government that is leading us in wartime." Moyers tells of how Walter Isaacson, then the head of CNN, had sent a memo (leaked to *The Washington Post*) prior to the Iraq invasion, instructing producers to "balance" any upsetting images of civilian casualties in Afghanistan with reminders about the horrors of 9/11; Isaacson would later acknowledge to Moyers that "we didn't question our sources enough" about the rationale for war. *Times* pundits, particularly Bill Kristol and William Safire, were pushing hard for "regime change" in Iraq, despite the country's lack of a direct connection to 9/11; it was long overdue, they wrote in op-ed columns and urged, endlessly, on TV talk shows. Editorial pages got behind the looming war, too, with *The Washington Post* taking a particularly hawkish stance.

Opinion journalism was one thing; hard-news reporting should have been another. But too often it wasn't. In story after story, at *The New York Times, The Washington Post,* and elsewhere, anonymous government sources confirmed this line of coverage. Any reporting that questioned it or applied due skepticism was given far less prominence. In his memoir, *All About the Story,* the former *Washington Post* editor Leonard Downie, Jr., admitted what he termed "my biggest mistakes as executive editor." He looked back at the news coverage from before the war and concluded that while there were some skeptical stories about the administration's hawkish claims, they were mostly relegated to the paper's inside pages. In newsroom parlance, they got buried. "Thinking like an editor, rather than as a reader, I too often assumed they could easily be found by readers in the multipage packages of prewar stories inside the newspaper's front—or 'A'—section each day," Downie wrote. "That was a mistake."

In the *Times,* one byline stood out and has become infamous as a symbol of the media's overall too-credible coverage: that of Judith Miller, a star reporter in the Washington bureau. Time after time, her articles appeared on the paper's front page, sourced anonymously and underscoring the administration's war-hungry justifications. In her 2015 book, *A Reporter's Journey,* Miller admits she got the weapons of mass destruction story wrong, but claims it wasn't because she was spoon-fed her conclusions by the administration; rather, it was because her high-level sources were wrong. (Although Miller's name is synonymous with some of the flawed prewar reporting, her career was varied, to say the least. Part of a Pulitzer Prize–winning team exploring the roots of terrorism in the wake of 9/11, she also spent months in a Virginia jail for refusing to reveal a source, left the *Times* in 2005, later contributed to Fox News and Newsmax, and became a fellow at the conservative Manhattan Institute.)

As Moyers pointed out in "Buying the War," the journalists in the Washington bureau of the Knight-Ridder papers were an admirable rarity; their reporting stood out for its dogged skepticism about the Bush administration's claims. Jonathan Landay and Warren Strobel got the story right. But because Knight-Ridder had no newspapers in New York or Washington, their reporting didn't resonate widely. It certainly didn't have anything close to the impact of a front-page article in the *Times*. Discussing it, Landay told CTV how lonely it was when he and Strobel were "questioning why no one else was reporting what we were reporting." Journalists, after all, are not supposed to be stenographers, just transmitting what an administration wants them to. Of course, eventually it became well known that these connections between Saddam and Al-Qaeda were a mirage, as was the existence of weapons of mass destruction. It was engineered by the war-hungry Bush administration and eagerly believed by a press that failed to do its basic job.

In a lengthy editor's note in 2004, the *Times* cast blame on itself for that pre-war coverage, saying in part:

> We have found a number of instances of coverage that was not as rigorous as it should have been. In some cases, information that was controversial then, and seems questionable now, was insufficiently qualified or allowed to stand unchallenged. Looking back, we wish we had been more aggressive in re-examining the claims as new evidence emerged—or failed to emerge.

It was quite a mea culpa, though it stopped short of an apology. The press's failure of skepticism took a toll on public trust. It was one of many factors—but an important one—in the way trust plummeted in the early years of the twenty-first century.

The numbers from Gallup, the opinion pollsters, tell the story vividly. In 2005, the level of public trust in the news media (those saying they trusted the media a great deal or a fair amount) dropped to 50 percent; it had been steadily falling from its height of 72 percent in 1976, in the post-Watergate era and, perhaps coincidentally, the year that *All the President's Men* came out. By 2007 (the year that Moyers's "Buying the War" aired on TV), public trust in the news media had dropped to 47 percent. It would continue to fall. Of course, the reasons are complicated; for one thing, trust in many other institutions was also on the wane. It's not possible to point to the misleading reporting in the Iraq War run-up and say definitively, "This is why." But it was certainly part of the problem, one that's been hard to recover from. Once public trust is betrayed, it's almost impossible to regain it.

Given all of this in the background, but far from forgotten, I was gratified by the reforms. My criticism of anonymous sources had been a years-long project—including my AnonyWatch gimmick on Twitter, in which I asked readers to keep track of the use of unnamed sources as they saw them and to tweet them out or point them out to me in an email. In March 2016, a couple of months after the San Bernardino debacle, when the changes were announced, I was nearly ready to wrap up my public editor stint. I allowed myself to think that, maybe, I had done some lasting good. Not only for *Times* readers, but for the health of the media ecosystem overall, which is so profoundly affected by the ever-influential *New York Times*.

Did the new policy stick or did the *Times* backslide? It wasn't encouraging to know that this wasn't the first time that the rules had been tightened, seemingly to no avail. As mentioned earlier, editors instituted stricter policies on the use of unnamed sources after the Iraq War lead-up. That had been more than a decade earlier, but based on what anyone could see, the crackdown had proved largely toothless. After the new reforms in early 2016, I continued to see reporting based on unnamed sources, which was no surprise—and not necessarily a bad thing. Such sourcing will always be necessary; it's a question of how widespread it is and how much rigorous skepticism is applied to what these sources are selling.

Since then, the *Times* endured a major reputation-damaging debacle, in which the main source for its acclaimed and award-winning podcast *Caliphate* was given a pseudonym and allowed to spin lies about his supposed radicalization by the Islamic State. The spellbinding podcast, which began in 2018, had made a superstar of its main reporter, Rukmini Callimachi, whose journalistic focus for years had been Islamic extremism. In 2020, the whole thing fell apart—the source's story was revealed to be largely a hoax—and the *Times* had to retract the core of the podcast's findings and return a Peabody Award. Callimachi was reassigned, but Baquet chose not to blame her publicly; he called it an institutional failing, not that of one reporter. Baquet was clear about what had happened internally, telling NPR's David Folkenflik: "We fell in love with the fact that we had gotten a member of ISIS who would describe his life in the caliphate and would describe his crimes. I think we were so in love with it that when we saw evidence that maybe he was a fabulist, when we saw evidence that he was making some of it up, we didn't listen hard enough."

This was a different kind of problem than the anonymous government reporting in the run-up to the Iraq War, but they had something in common: Proper skepticism was missing. Clearly this problem hadn't gone away. Nevertheless, even now, I allow myself to hope that the stricter rules I pushed for have prevented a journalistic disaster or two that would have cut further into public trust. One commenter on my 2016 column about the new anonymous-sources policy echoed the doubt I expressed about how thoroughly it would be carried out in the long run, writing: "Sadly, Sullivan's skepticism carries more weight than Baquet's proclamation. If the Judith Miller episode, and other serious failures due to anonymous sourcing from many years past, weren't enough to make the policy stick, I'm less than confident we'll be seeing it vigorously enforced a couple of years from now when this deep addiction's suppressed cravings rise up again. If this new resolve does last, however, it will be thanks to a combination of Ms. Sullivan's persistent efforts and the loud objections of readers over the years who have tried to save the credibility and effectiveness of the country's best paper, and will be this Public Editor's most important legacy." For a brief moment, I felt as if Sisyphus had managed to keep the boulder balanced—however precariously—at the top of the mountain.

8

Moving On

Well into my third year at the *Times*, with less than one year to go, Arthur Sulzberger asked me to come up to his office on the thirteenth floor. This was highly unusual, and I wondered whether there was something unpleasant to discuss. Was I being sued? Fired? Taken to the woodshed? But no, it was quite the opposite. The *Times* publisher was happy with my work and wanted to invite me to stay longer than the four-year term we had agreed upon in 2012. I wasn't completely surprised by this development. While the *Times* newsroom, its editors and reporters, may not have enjoyed my scrutiny and sometimes my criticism, the publisher—who was a step above and apart from the fray—actually liked it when I wrote tough columns, as long as he considered them fair. After all, he had agreed to start the position in order to hold the institution accountable to its own standards; in some ways, he felt the public editor role was his baby, if not his brainchild. Clearly, he thought I was doing what I'd been hired to do. Now he wanted me to stay for another term of perhaps two more years, for a total of six; we never got far enough in the conversation to iron out such details because I indicated fairly quickly that I didn't think it was a good idea. And I told him why I thought so: The whole notion of the public editor's role requires the person doing it to be something of an outsider. But after three years of arriving at 620 Eighth Avenue, seeing the same writers and editors every day—usually on a friendly and collegial basis—and eating in the same cafeteria, I was starting to lose the outsider's mentality. Or at least I feared I was. I tried to guard against it in my work. Even a four-year term would be longer than any of my four predecessors had stayed.

Another reason I thought it was getting to be time to go was that it was seductive being a part of this important news organization, even if my role was a peculiar one. Like few other institutions—Harvard comes to mind as comparable—the *Times* has a singular kind of cachet. People tend to be impressed when you say you work there. I had done my best to resist that, too. Still, four years would be more than enough; in fact, three might have been a wiser limit.

But the old how-to-make-a-living question soon arose: If not another term as public editor, then what? At this point, I was well into my fifties, and I knew that being an older woman isn't an ideal condition for job hunting, especially in the ever-more-digital media realm. The sooner I made a move, I thought, the better. So I started to put out some feelers. As soon as I did, I realized that the past three years as public editor had put me in a strong position for job hunting. I had been on the national stage, and people knew my name and generally liked my work. I started hearing about some jobs at regional news organizations, even a top editor's job at one of the largest newspapers in the country. That was a great opportunity for someone, no doubt, but it was not something that I found particularly appealing. After all, I had had the privilege, for more than twelve years, of running the single local newsroom that I loved, the one at *The Buffalo News*, where the staff seemed almost like my family. Maybe it was too sentimental, but it struck me as almost disloyal to go across the country to a similar job elsewhere.

And I hated the thought of leaving New York City, which, from the moment I moved there, felt like my spiritual home. I'd made new friends, developed a social life, even bought an apartment on the Upper West Side. How could I leave my book loft, my walks in Central Park, the sense of good fortune I had when I realized that I had become a New Yorker, sharing geography if not talent with so many of the writers—past and present—I admired? And, after all, there were certainly lots of opportunities in New York, the media home of the nation, if not the world.

I had started to think about going to *The Washington Post*, the legendary newspaper that had first piqued my interest in journalism through the Watergate reporting of Bob Woodward and Carl Bernstein. I knew and admired Marty Baron, who had been named the top editor there just a couple of years before; he arrived before Amazon founder Jeff Bezos bought the paper from the Graham family for $250 million. Baron was revered in the news business for the journalism he had led at the *Miami Herald* and *The Boston Globe* (later immortalized in the Oscar-winning film *Spotlight*, in which he was played by a taciturn but inspirational Liev Schreiber). He was well known at the *Times*, too, where he worked for several years. *Times* people tended to remember him as a particularly demanding editor, a stickler for quality and journalistic rigor, no matter who might be (unapologetically) inconvenienced or how late at night such an inconvenience might happen. Marty didn't seem to care whom he annoyed when he was dissatisfied with a piece of journalism. He had even been in touch with me in my role as public editor in early 2014 to complain about the *Times* not giving adequate credit to the *Post* for its reporting. I had quoted him in a public editor's blog post, sounding clearly dissatisfied with the lack of adequate response from *Times* editors. In his email to me, he detailed a number of instances that perturbed him, suggesting that getting in touch with me was something of a last resort: "In each instance, we informed key *Times* editors that our previous reporting, often many months in advance, went uncredited. We either never heard back or were dismissed." I took Baron's complaints to Phil Corbett, the standards editor, who gave me a detailed and thoughtful response, without quite saying the *Times* had been in the wrong. I later heard that this kind of public complaint from a colleague and a high-ranking peer didn't sit particularly well with Dean Baquet, who counted Baron as a close friend. It's hard to imagine too many other top editors making such a complaint to a *New York Times* ombudsman, but it was in character for Marty.

At the *Post,* Baron already had made his mark, and he did it quickly; in 2014, the paper shared journalism's highest honor, the Pulitzer Prize for Public Service, with *The Guardian* for their reporting on the Snowden revelations. It took guts to do that kind of consequential work.

I didn't consider Baron a friend, exactly, but we knew each other a bit, ever since the days when I was editor of *The*

Buffalo News. So I got in touch with Marty and asked him if he'd have lunch with me in Washington. I said I hoped to ask his advice about my next move after the *Times.* He readily agreed, and we met on a Saturday at a casual restaurant not far from where he lived. Over lunch, I told him about the various leads I had on jobs and revealed my ulterior motive for the lunch: I asked him if he'd consider creating a new position at the *Post,* that of media columnist, modeled after the widely admired column that David Carr had written before his sudden death. This would be a reported column, not pure opinion, and it would be, according to my pitch, housed on the news side of the *Post,* not in its editorial section with the prominent op-ed columnists like Eugene Robinson and E. J. Dionne. I made it clear that I no longer wanted to be an ombudsman or public editor, and I knew that that wasn't an option at the *Post;* the paper, like a growing number of other news organizations around the country, had eliminated that position a few years earlier, much to its readers' unhappiness. I also said I saw myself writing in the Style section, which is devoted to arts and culture, not in the business section, as Carr had done.

Baron seemed at least moderately intrigued by my idea, and asked me to write a proposal describing how I'd approach the job and what it might produce. I did so, and he said he liked it; for someone whose demeanor and style of communication is famously low-key, this seemed almost enthusiastic. It certainly was encouraging. But I soon found out there was going to be far more to the process than the executive editor merely waving his hand and making it happen. There were editors—lots of editors—to meet and be interviewed by:

Kevin Merida, Cameron Barr, Tracy Grant, Liz Seymour, and David Malitz. As things progressed, Baron even had me meet with *Post* publisher Fred Ryan, once the chief of staff to former president Ronald Reagan and the co-founder of Politico, the D.C.–based news organization. During our cordial chat, Fred mentioned that he trusted I wouldn't turn myself into the *Post*'s ombudswoman after I got in the door. I didn't; if I'd wanted to be a public editor, I would have stayed at the *Times*.

In other words, I ran the full obstacle course. Finally, though, I had a firm job offer from the *Post*. Editors there, including Baron, preferred that I move to Washington permanently, but I didn't want to make that commitment and they didn't force the issue. Instead, I agreed to live in Washington for the first year, and after that, I would be free to move back to New York City. I hedged my bets on that by arranging to rent out my New York apartment but not to sell it. I didn't see myself falling out of love with New York City any time soon.

I was apprehensive about telling Sulzberger about my decision to leave the *Times*, especially because my four-year term wouldn't be complete until the summer; I intended to start at the *Post* a few months before that. I made another visit to his thirteenth-floor office, and broke the news. (It reminded me of another elevator ride to another publisher's office four years earlier, when I told my longtime boss in Buffalo, Stan Lipsey, that I was headed to *The New York Times*.) Sulzberger was completely gracious, though I didn't know that right away, since his first words were, "That damn Marty Baron! I'll never forgive him for this." He was kidding, though, and seemed genuinely pleased for me—and for Marty, whom he knew well from his stint at the *Times*. This was in keeping with my whole experience with Sulzberger, whose treatment of me as public editor was close to ideal. He was supportive of my work, even when it was harshly critical of his paper, and he gave me complete independence, never trying to intrude or to suggest what I could or couldn't write about. I know he was less than happy about some very early columns in which I questioned the *Times*'s hiring of CEO Mark Thompson, who had been embroiled in the aftermath of a scandal at the BBC, where he had been director general. Just before Thompson started the *Times* CEO job, I wrote: "His integrity and decision-making are bound to affect The Times and its journalism—profoundly. It's worth considering now whether he is the right person for the job." One of the New York City tabloids referred to me, in a big headline, as the "Thompson Gunner." This business-side move was arguably none of my business as public editor, and caused plenty of raised eyebrows inside the newsroom. To his credit, Sulzberger never told me to knock it off, though he did mention, quite mildly, that he would have appreciated some notice about what I was planning.

As I prepared to leave in 2016, Sulzberger did make one request: Would I stay through the presidential election and into early 2017, when a new president would be inaugurated? He thought it important to have an experienced public editor at such a critical time. I told him that I would think about it. In the end, though, it seemed as though it would be awkward, and potentially a conflict of interest, to stay around for another nine months when I knew I would soon be going to work for one of the *Times*'s chief competitors. So I declined his offer with sincere thanks and made my plans to wrap up my public editor stint and move to Washington.

Later, though, especially given the extremely consequential news events near the close of the 2016 presidential campaign, I wondered if my decision had been a selfish one. Certainly, it was driven in part by my desire to move forward to the next challenge—and not to be unemployed for even a short time. Living in New York City was not something I wanted to do without a steady paycheck. But maybe I should have simply waited. I consoled myself with the knowledge that even if I had served every minute of my four-year term, I still would have been gone from the *Times* by October 2016, a particularly crucial moment in the presidential campaign news cycle. That was when FBI director James Comey decided to reopen the investigation into Hillary Clinton's email practices, and when the *Times* overplayed that story, giving over the entire top of its front page to it just days before the presidential election.

At any rate, I harbored no illusions about being irreplaceable. I knew there were plenty of journalists out there who could do the public editor job as well or better than I had. Still, it was gratifying, and humbling, to hear how much readers had appreciated my work.

My departure had brought what one of my *Times* assistants, Jonah Bromwich, called "a standing ovation." One reader, whose handle was Dotconnector, contributed a comment on my last column: "What readers want most from the *Times* is for it to be true to its oft-stated values, and no one has ever given voice to our concerns about that more effectively than Ms. Sullivan. There simply never has been a more devoted—or prolific—reader advocate anywhere." I smiled at Dotconnector's allusion to the Carly Simon song "Nobody Does It Better."

I was glad to see that the *Times* soon hired a well-qualified person, Liz Spayd—a former *Washington Post* managing editor who had become the editor and publisher of *Columbia Journalism Review*—to be its sixth public editor. Once she got started, I admired some of her columns and disagreed with others. Because I knew firsthand what a fraught relationship existed between the public editor and the *Times* staff, I wasn't shocked when, only thirteen months later, the *Times* announced that it was eliminating the public editor's position altogether. The *Times*'s leadership said that Twitter and other forms of social media were supplying plenty of outside criticism, making an internal voice to represent the readers no longer necessary. Instead, there would be a new "Reader Center" to serve as a clearinghouse for complaints and to respond to criticism.

I thought that ending the public editor position was a serious mistake. I knew from experience that the job wasn't just about criticizing the paper; it was also about investigating problems and complaints, and getting answers from the decision-makers to relay to the readers. Twitter can't do that. But by then, this wasn't really my problem. I was already immersed in my work at *The Washington Post*, where, given the state of national politics, there was no shortage of all-consuming drama. Still, I was sad about it and, to some extent, I took it personally. If I had really been effective, wouldn't the job have seemed too valuable to toss out? As public trust in the news media declined, I knew that the continuing loss of these reader representatives at news organizations all over the country was a step in the wrong direction.

Shortly before I left, and after my new job at the *Post* had been announced publicly, Arthur Sulzberger organized a farewell dinner for me in a private room at Barbetta, an elegant theater-district restaurant within walking distance of the *Times*. The attendees were many of the same *Times* editors whom I had been publicly criticizing for more than three years. Conversation didn't exactly flow, since subject matter was limited. They couldn't freely talk shop with me present, especially since I was about to become a media writer at one of their biggest competitors. With both the publisher and the public editor present, newsroom gossip was off-limits. And some of them, no doubt, were still stinging from things I had written about them or their staffs in the recent past, perhaps feeling I had treated them unfairly or embarrassed them publicly. I couldn't imagine they were sorry to see me wrap things up, though I think most of them liked me well enough on a strictly personal level. In short, it was a bit awkward. Sulzberger led a toast to me, and the editors' glasses were raised, whether reluctantly or enthusiastically. We all got through it somehow, but like so many of my *New York Times* experiences, the farewell dinner was more than a little uncomfortable. I looked forward to being a real part of a newsroom again, not a critical outsider.

Much more fun was a final dinner with the young assistants who had served me so well. Only one, Joseph Burgess, was missing, since he had moved to California. But the other four were there: Meghan Gourley, Jonah Bromwich, Joumana Khatib, and Evan Gershkovich. All, I knew, were headed for great things or already achieving them, and that faith has been borne out. (By 2022, Bromwich was a *Times* courts reporter, Khatib an editor in the *Times* book review section, Gourley at Microsoft in Seattle, Burgess a veteran of *Apple News,* and Gershkovich—remarkably—was reporting from Moscow for *The Wall Street Journal* as Russia invaded Ukraine.) In honor of my and Joumana's heritage, we went to Ilili, a Lebanese restaurant on Fifth Avenue in the Flatiron District, not far from where I had lived when I moved to New York in 2012. After dinner, I asked a bystander to photograph the five of us. The street scene in that image has a film-noir feeling that captured my melancholy mood. I loved these brilliant young people and I felt real regret to be leaving them, and New York City, behind.

9

The Joys of Style

Whatever my regrets were about leaving New York City, it was exciting to be working at *The Washington Post.* And it was especially thrilling to be in the Style section, which the legendary editor Ben Bradlee had invented decades before as a much edgier successor to the traditional and predictable "women's section" of the paper, devoted to society news and homemaking tips. I'd been reading and admiring Style for a long time, as far back as when I was in college at Georgetown and the *Post* was my local paper, along with the now-defunct *Washington Star,* whose gossip column, "The Ear," was always a delicious read.

I loved the section's clever, often daring, writers, who brought a literary sensibility—and fearlessness—to their work. Among them: Judith Martin (who later became "Miss Manners," the arch and addictively readable etiquette columnist), Henry Allen, Sally Quinn, Stephanie Mansfield, Martha Sherrill, and—perhaps the greatest of all—Marjorie Williams, a sparkling writer who specialized in subtly devastating profiles of politicians, and who died far too early of cancer.

I also loved the section's history of taking chances, turning phrases, and annoying the Washington establishment. That tension was memorably depicted in the 2017 Steven Spielberg movie *The Post,* about the fraught decision to publish the Pentagon Papers in the early 1970s after *The New York Times* was temporarily stopped from publishing by a restraining order from the Nixon administration. Gorgeously played by Meryl Streep, the newspaper's publisher, Katharine Graham, mildly scolds Bradlee about his brainchild of a new section after getting a complaint from none other than President Nixon himself, who, even well before Watergate, considered the *Post* his nemesis. "I'm not sure I entirely blame the president on this one, Ben," Streep (aka Graham) pointedly tells her editor. "Would you want Judith [Martin] to cover *your* daughter's wedding? . . . She compared Tricia Nixon to a vanilla ice-cream cone." Graham, a social doyenne as well as a powerful businesswoman, wondered whether this journalistic experiment of Bradlee's was really turning out to be such a smart idea: "Sometimes that stiletto party coverage can be a little mean," she rebuked him. Bradlee, played by Tom Hanks, found it necessary to push back and assert editorial independence. "Katharine," he responded, "keep your finger out of my eye." Ultimately, she did just that, and continued to give free rein and plentiful support to Bradlee and his journalists. The section and its writers endured, and its blend of arts criticism and scintillating feature writing set the standard for American newspapers.

One of the reasons the section meant so much to me was that, as a young editor at *The Buffalo News*, I had founded a new section myself—also a successor to the paper's women's section—that was modeled on Style. At the *News,* we called our new section Life & Arts. I was still on maternity leave with my first child when I started envisioning it, but I nevertheless made arrangements to spend a day visiting the *Post* to talk with the Style editors, including the top section editor, Mary Hadar. While visiting the newsroom, in the old building, which I had seen before only in *All the President's Men,* I had the chance to sit in on a front-page planning meeting with Bradlee at the helm. He was making wisecracks and looking just as dashing as I'd imagined, even though he was nearly seventy years old. He paid little attention to me, a fledgling editor from the provinces. It all made for a never-to-be-forgotten day, though not really a pleasant one. I had given birth to Alex just a few months earlier and was still breast-feeding him full-time. That meant we couldn't be separated for very long. So I brought him down to Washington, where a friend took care of him in her northern Virginia apartment while I spent the day at the *Post.* I remember trying to use a clear plastic breast pump in one of the restroom stalls between meetings with editors, but feeling so much stress in the unfamiliar surroundings that I finally gave up. This was awkward and physically uncomfortable, and I couldn't wait to leave the newspaper's office and get back to my friend's place. After our longest-ever separation, Alex was more than ready to see me, too. There would be many times over the years that my personal life and professional ambitions would conflict, or even collide, and this certainly was one of them.

Now, more than twenty-five years after that visit—Alex had graduated from law school—it was time to show that I belonged in Style as a full-time writer, not just as a random visitor from another paper. But *did* I belong? In my early weeks at the *Post,* I had my doubts. Sitting in story-brainstorming meetings with reporters and editors, I didn't feel like I had much to offer. These were journalists who had been at the *Post* for years, who had put the special Style spin on members of Congress, First Ladies, media types, lobbyists, and fixtures of Washington society, from JFK, Jr., to Barbara Bush. They knew all the gossip about who used to be married to whom, and why that famous Washington lawyer fell from grace. I was having some trouble adjusting. One would have thought that the much more difficult transition would have come four years earlier when I left Buffalo and my top editor's job for *The New York Times,* but that went swimmingly from the start. It wasn't easy, but everything just clicked. That wasn't happening in Washington, not at first.

I felt the pressure of high expectations; I was a marquee hire for the *Post*'s top editor, Marty Baron, which meant I had a lot to prove. He was watching, I knew, and so were all the people who had read my *Times* work over the past four years. My profile was high because of the very visible role of the *Times* public editor. When I was hired at the *Post,* one media website wrote about how the paper had hired me before my term was up, "in a pre-emptive move." Now that I was here, I had to perform. On my first day at the *Times,* I had written a successful blog post that set the tone for my entire stint there. But at the *Post,* I spent my first day in an hours-long meeting about a clunky, non-intuitive "content management system" annoyingly called Méthode. That training was the kind of thing I detested; it made my head hurt. I went home that first night to my underfurnished studio apartment in a nondescript building near the National Mall and flopped face-first onto my bed. What was I doing here, alone, starting a daunting new job well into my fifties? I was having serious doubts about the choice I'd made, and I was feeling the pressure to prove myself. Soon.

Even working in Style—that section I had admired for so long and imagined myself a part of—had one drawback. If you weren't a Washington insider and a regular reader of the print paper, the name was confusing. It was hard, sometimes, to explain to readers who didn't know the history of Style why my work, often sharply opinionated about politics and critical of the media, appeared in a section that sounded like a fashion magazine. Some of them wondered: Had I gone from being a tough-minded public editor to writing froth about hemlines? So I explained, over and over (as did my brilliant new colleagues like Dan Zak, Monica Hesse, Paul Farhi, Ben Terris, and Ann Hornaday), that the section was, and always had been, about the arts, politics, media, and the broader culture. Our part of the newsroom was abundantly populated with Pulitzer Prize winners: the art critic Phil Kennicott, the dance critic Sarah Kaufman, the fashion and social critic Robin Givhan. Political cartoonist Tom Toles, who had been my colleague in Buffalo before succeeding the *Post*'s legendary Herblock, was a regular presence, and the book critic Carlos Lozada would stop by to chat with the savvy Book World staff, like my podmates Steve Levingston and Nora Krug.

Stimulating as all of this was, I felt out of place. All of a sudden, after being a top boss and then having an important role at the *Times,* I was a writer again—a "humble scribe," in the self-mocking parlance of the newsroom—although at a legendary publication that was having another moment in the zeitgeist. My new role meant that for the first time in more than twenty years, I was without an office of my own, without an assistant, and without a single person who reported to me. My desk was out in the newsroom, where I was elbow to elbow with other writers and editors, overhearing them on the phone, just as they could do with me if anyone wanted to bother. I wasn't completely comfortable with the sudden lack of privacy and hierarchical status, but I've always loved the ambiance of any newsroom, whether at the *Niagara Gazette* or the grand *New York Times:* the wised-up attitudes, the practical jokes, the shared history of past moments of glory or embarrassment, the sense of having a front-row seat for unfolding history. Sitting in on those brainstorming meetings with my new *Post* colleagues, I was daunted. I found one of the editors, Amy Argetsinger, downright intimidating because she seemed so breezily knowledgeable about Washington personalities and their history; she had been the author of the *Post*'s gossip column for a few years. (In time, she would become my direct editor, someone who sharpened my copy immensely.) But I didn't yet feel I had much to contribute, though they seemed happy to have me there. I kept hearing how much my new colleagues had admired my work at the *Times*—but that was then. For once in my life, I was mostly keeping my mouth shut.

For a journalist, this particular newsroom was an exalted place. The *Post* had moved into a glitzy new building just before my arrival. Gone was the cluttered 1970s-style newsroom that the movie version of *All the President's Men* had copied so faithfully, with its phones ringing and typewriters clattering. Instead, I saw acres of glass walls, quiet "huddle rooms," and, etched on the walls, inspiring quotations from people like Ben Bradlee, Katharine Graham, and, yes, the *Post*'s new owner, Jeff Bezos. The founder of Amazon and one of the richest people in the world, Bezos had bought the paper from the Graham family in 2013 and had ambitious plans for its resurgence and for national—even global—prominence and reach. I liked Bradlee's quote, in particular: "The truth, no matter how bad, is never as dangerous as a lie in the long run." The place was quiet—no loud typewriters or phones ringing off the hook—but still bursting with energy. It was palpable in the air, and for good reason. Unlike almost every other newspaper in the country in 2016, the *Post* was growing, not shrinking. It felt ambitious, urgent, forward-leaning. If the newspaper industry, in general, was in retreat because of failing finances, the *Post* was doing the opposite under its billionaire owner: charging determinedly ahead. Compared to the *Times* newsroom, which I had just left, the *Post*'s felt edgier, less self-satisfied, with a sense of seizing this moment by the throat and not letting go. It reminded me of the old advertising line from the car rental company Avis, always comparing itself to the market leader Hertz: "We're number two. We try harder."

Although it was hard for me to readjust to working in the trenches again, I was extremely lucky in one regard: the particular journalists who sat around me. The great book critic Ron Charles, whose reviews I had admired for years, was mere feet away, and he was as funny, kind, and charming as could be hoped. Across from me was Julia Carpenter, who—although she was thirty years my junior—turned out to be a kindred spirit; we shared a fervent admiration for writers like Joan Didion, Nora Ephron, and Laurie Colwin. Julia was a great help as I figured out how to function in this new environment. She was one of the digital-audience experts who had been strategically placed around the newsroom where they could have a subtle (or in my case, not so subtle) influence on how our work was presented to the public.

When I wrote my first media column for the *Post*—an argument that journalism, though troubled, was still a good field for young people to enter as a career—I was told to put my own proposed headline on it for an editor to consider and possibly change. Peering over the short wall between our desks, I asked Julia if she had any thoughts on a headline; she quickly took a read and then introduced me to the fine art of the one-two punch headline: two brief sentences or phrases meant to engage readers with a conversational tone and, by introducing an element of mystery, to lure them into reading an article. Not meant to be clickbait, but serving as an intriguing invitation. What she suggested ended up as the published headline: "Now, There's One More Reason to Be a Journalist—You Can Help Save Journalism." This first column of mine was not exactly a hard-hitting piece; it was far from the most provocative column I would write at the *Post* or what editors wanted from me, though they didn't complain. The entertaining and incisive media critic for Politico, Jack Shafer, took a good-natured swipe at it, tweeting that my first *Post* column was "marred by optimism." He needn't have been concerned about this rosy outlook enduring for long; my point of view—on journalism but also on national politics and the direction of American society in general—would get darker and darker as the months went by, particularly as 2016 presidential politics moved fully onto center stage.

It took me several weeks, which felt like centuries, to begin to hit my stride. I recognized that my first few columns, while not disastrous, had missed the mark. One longtime reader of mine, a fan of my *Times* writing, emailed to tell me of his disappointment: "You used to be funny. You're not funny anymore." He had a good point; I hadn't found my voice, something that had come so easily to me as public editor. And even though I had gone to college in Washington and had lived there briefly one other time, I wasn't feeling at home in the District. I adored New York. When I moved downstate in 2012 to become the *Times* public editor, I walked around feeling thrilled. New York City fed my soul. Washington had a lot going for it—arts and culture, a burgeoning restaurant scene, and hip neighborhoods—but somehow it didn't really suit me. The man I was madly in love with referred to it with the disparaging nickname of "SACT": sterile, anodyne company town. I missed the more eclectic, grittier, glamorous city I'd just moved away from. I missed my Upper West Side apartment with its book-lined loft and its proximity to Central Park. And I'd left a relationship behind—to be continued, or maybe not. As usual, I hadn't made my decisions with my personal life at the top of the agenda. All of this was wrenching. But the writing difficulties, at least, were short-lived.

I realized soon that I had underestimated—simply didn't *get*—how thoroughly *The Washington Post* was concerned with national politics. You could almost say that, for the *Post* and its readers, there really was no other topic. It was the subject on which the *Post* had long excelled, where it had the most expertise—consider Watergate and, more recently, the stunning revelations from the government whistleblower Edward Snowden. National politics was what readers everywhere came to the *Post* looking for. I quickly found out that writing about anything else simply wouldn't get the job done.

Eventually I got the drift. I saw an opportunity to hit hard when CNN made the terrible decision to hire Corey Lewandowski as one of their talking-head pundits. Lewandowski, the former Trump campaign manager, had repeatedly shown himself to be a bully and an opponent of the legitimate press. He had even been arrested by Florida police after a reporter covering Trump claimed he had roughed her up; Lewandowski denied it, but one of my colleagues had witnessed it firsthand. (The charges were eventually dropped after prosecutors said there was "probable cause" to move forward but insufficient evidence to get a conviction.)

Several weeks into the job, I finally wound up my fastball. My column began: "Even in the highly competitive, ratings-mad, hardball-playing world of cable television, there should be a bridge too far. In hiring Donald Trump's fired campaign manager Corey Lewandowski, CNN ran blithely across that bridge and plunged into a sea of muck." My journal for that day makes note, with some relief, of the positive reaction: that Marty Baron "actually emailed to call it spot-on" and that the NYU professor and press critic Jay Rosen had tweeted that *this* was what he was hoping for when I moved to the *Post.* The clear implication, a little tough to take in, was that the Lewandowski column was the first time that Jay, who had become a friend in New York, was seeing any evidence of those hopes coming to fruition.

From that point on, I recognized that I needed to write nimbly and with a harder, more critical edge. I needed to react quickly to the immediate news of the day as national politics intersected with the news media. A couple of weeks later, on July 5, 2016—shortly before the national political conventions—I took on Hillary Clinton with a column about how she had been stonewalling the press during her presidential campaign, especially since she had tried to defend her email practices in a news conference widely seen as a bust. I had written, of course, about the Clinton-email story line quite a bit at the *Times,* so this was familiar territory. This column began:

> Remember Fort Dodge, Iowa? No? Well, that's understandable. It's been a long time—seven months—since an event in Fort Dodge that turned out to be historic: Hillary Clinton's last news conference. The candidate, famously opaque, answered a grand total of seven questions there on Dec. 4, 2015. Since then, although she's given individual interviews, she hasn't made herself available for general media questioning.

I concluded with a strong push for more transparency from Clinton, the woman whom just about everyone at that point—myself included—considered to be the president-in-waiting: "This can't go on. It's not just time for a full-length, no-holds-barred news conference. It's way past time."

As I made the rocky adjustment from public editor to media columnist, my direct editor, Richard Leiby, a newsroom character of the old-school variety, was a help. Well, mostly. A former Pakistan correspondent for the *Post,* Leiby is a wordsmith with deep institutional knowledge of the *Post* and of Washington. A clever writer himself, he would sometimes suggest a pithy phrase for my column that ended up being quoted and admired; I tried not to take the credit even though it was under my byline. We got along well, but our metabolisms were radically different in a way that I sometimes found frustrating. I was revved up: I would file my column in the morning, reacting to some news event, and would want to get it published as soon as possible. Realizing how important timeliness was, I had a sense of urgency, maybe more than was strictly necessary. I knew that publishing early in the day would mean that more readers would likely see it, and I wanted to take advantage of that. Unlike a lot of newspapers, which were still adjusting to the decline of print, the *Post* was oriented almost entirely toward the online audience. The priority of engaging that audience was built right into the goals we were urged to meet in our work: to be nimble and innovative, always. It was *Post* policy that stories always published online first; the printed newspaper, while not exactly an afterthought, was definitely secondary.

Leiby, who had seen it all before, was much more relaxed

than I and would often interrupt our editing sessions to introduce off-the-subject questions or stories that made me dig my fingernails into my palms in frustration. "Did I ever tell you about the time I nearly led the Iraq army?" he would ask about once a month, while we were on deadline. He also made some gentle fun of my idealistic views about the role of the press in American society, teasing that I ought to have a special key on my computer to insert a few ready-made, often-repeated lines about how journalism exists to hold elected officials accountable to citizens and how the press is a bulwark of our democracy. The most important thing was that he was careful and wise, and on one occasion when a column of mine was unfairly challenged by a source, he was adamant—and successful—in defending it.

There were layers upon layers of editors. Leiby reported to one of my favorite people, David Malitz, a young former music critic with impeccable journalistic judgment. And Malitz, in turn, reported to the whip-smart Liz Seymour, who as the top editor of the features department had the same job I had held for a long time in Buffalo—except she supervised a much larger staff. All of this made me start to feel like I was in the right place.

I didn't have a great deal of contact with Marty Baron, but when I did, it could be memorable. One time I sent the famously rigorous editor a draft version of a column I was working on (he had suggested the topic) and asked if he had any thoughts. I got back an incredibly detailed note, with suggestions about sources to talk to, other angles to take, problems with what I'd written so far, and some copy editing, down to the errant semicolon. It was all on point and useful—Marty is a top-flight editor—but I didn't often go down the road of sending him a column in advance. Occasionally he would send me a complimentary email, or even recommend my column on his personal Twitter feed. When that happened, I felt as though I could take the rest of the week off. Luckily, I suppose, it didn't happen all that often.

The *Post*'s top editor had far bigger things to think about than his new media columnist. Under Bezos's ownership and Marty's leadership, the paper was thriving and finding some of the moxie, so abundant in the Watergate era, that had been far less apparent in recent years when it was laying off staff and trimming back its ambitions. In those years, revenue dwindled and circulation fell, though it was still making a profit. Now, with this billionaire owner and his high-flying goals for glory and success (both journalistically and business-wise), it was a new day altogether. Marty was an editor who had elevated the journalism at every place he'd worked, particularly when he'd led the newsrooms at the *Miami Herald* and *The Boston Globe*, picking up Pulitzer Prizes along the way like loaves of bread at the supermarket. He made his mark almost immediately at the *Post* by directing the reporting based on former NSA contractor Edward Snowden's top-secret revelations about how the government, in the wake of 9/11, was surveilling its own citizens. It was a major scoop (done in concert with the American arm of the British *Guardian*), one that was especially gratifying since *The New York Times*, the *Post*'s major competitor, often jokingly referred to in the newsroom as "Brand X," didn't have the Snowden story and had to play catch-up. In the competitive world of journalism, not much is sweeter than that.

Bezos wasn't the *Post*'s owner yet when Marty was hired by the Graham family member Katharine Weymouth in 2012. The Amazon founder bought the financially struggling paper the following year for only $250 million; the bargain price reflected just how besieged the newspaper industry had become. (For context, *The New York Times* had bought *The Boston Globe* in 1993 for $1.1 billion; those were still the days of fat profits for regional dailies. By 2013, when the *Times* sold the *Globe* to John Henry, owner of the Boston Red Sox, the price was only $70 million.) He had the good sense to recognize that he had precisely the right editor already in place. To his credit, Bezos didn't mess with success, and while some at the paper worried that such a dominant personality would intrude on editorial independence, he has—by all accounts I've ever heard—exerted his influence only on the business side of the operation, pushing the company to become ever more digital and to seek an ever-larger global audience.

Just a few months before I arrived, I watched from a distance as Bezos spoke to the staff at a celebration for the return of Jason Rezaian, the *Post* reporter who had been held captive for eighteen months in an Iranian prison; Baron had been a fierce and effective advocate for his release. Bezos had just flown Jason and his family home from Germany on his private jet, and everyone was in good spirits since there had been no guarantee that this happy reunion would ever take place. Some had thought Jason would never be released or might be killed.

The owner's words were memorable, and they established a tone for what he wanted the newsroom to be and do, a movement that was already well under way: "Even in the world of journalism, I think the *Post* is just a little more swashbuckling. There's a little more swagger. There's a tiny bit of *bad-assness* here at the *Post*." After some applause and laughs from the exuberant crowd, Bezos elaborated on those words with some context: "Without quality journalism, swashbuckling would just be dumb. Swashbuckling without professionalism leads to those epic-fail YouTube videos. It's the quality journalism at the heart of everything. And then when you add that swagger and that swashbuckling, that's making this place very, very special."

This was the *Washington Post* newsroom that I had just joined: a place that strived for both quality and swagger, with every chance of achieving that aim. I planned to do my part. And, as it turned out, I would get my chance, because the biggest story I had ever covered was coming at me like a speeding train.

10

"Venomous Serpent"

By the summer of 2016, the relationship between the American press and the American public had been deteriorating for many years. Trust had broken down; the general public's belief in journalism as a necessary good in society had plummeted since I fell under its spell as a teenager in the mid-1970s. I knew this, of course, after many years in local journalism and my stint at *The New York Times* fielding reader complaints.

Yet I was unprepared for the moment of no return that came on a hot July day in 2016, as a blazing sun beat down onto the streets of downtown Cleveland. I had a familiar anxious feeling as I walked around the grounds of the 2016 Republican National Convention, looking for a column idea. I had been working at *The Washington Post* as the media columnist for only a couple of months after my *Times* stint had concluded, and at this moment, as almost always in my life, I was experiencing the combined blessing and curse of my relentless internal drive to prove myself.

I was all too aware that I had started a new chapter of my life and career, and that the accolades I might have collected at the *Times* wouldn't last forever. Journalism is ephemeral, after all; even the best journalists of their day are quickly forgotten. (Just try asking a cross-section of today's journalism students about yesterday's greats, like the *Times* reporter David Halberstam, who distinguished himself with Vietnam War coverage in the 1960s, or Gene Roberts, who turned a regional paper, *The Philadelphia Inquirer,* into a Pulitzer Prize–winning machine in the 1970s and 1980s.) The reporter's bitter joke is that, even after the greatest scoop of all time, your editor will have only one thing to say: "What have you got for me today?"

I shouldn't have worried about finding material; the biggest story of my life was unfolding right there before my eyes. I just had to find my angle and a way to do justice to it. Wandering and observing in downtown Cleveland, I came upon a table of souvenirs, meant to appeal to the convention attendees who had arrived from all corners of the nation to cheer on the Republican Party's nomination of Donald Trump as their presidential candidate. I already had seen some nasty anti-Clinton signs and paraphernalia ("Hillary sucks but not like Monica" was one appalling meme.)

The gleeful misogyny was palpable. But nothing measured up to the horror I felt as I registered the meaning of a T-shirt featuring the image of a noose and these words: "Rope. Tree. Journalist. Some assembly required." The notion of death by lynching was meant to be funny, I guess, but the message was all too serious: We journalists were hated. Better off dead.

That ugly tone permeated the convention. Inside Cleveland's Quicken Loans Arena the next night, the crowd chanted, calling incessantly for the imprisonment of Hillary

Clinton—"Lock her up! Lock her up!"—as Donald Trump officially became the Republican nominee for president. Waves of disgust and anger came off the crowd, and Trump gloried in it. He hadn't invented any of this wretched emotion, of course, but he certainly emboldened, unleashed, and took advantage of it. As I started to write what I hoped were well-reasoned columns about Trump's relationship with the media, I continually felt that irrational anger like an unending blast of liquid poison from an industrial-strength hose.

On social media, and in phone messages and in emails I received, the sheer hatred from Trump supporters shocked and even frightened me. I had no choice but to send some of these incoming hate missives to the security department at *The Washington Post.* One, unsigned but from a "lifetime member of the NRA," informed me that people like me wouldn't be around much longer. Another, signed "A Real, True Patriot," was typical, and I think it's worth reproducing here at some length because it gives a sense of the tone, if not the volume, of what was coming at me.

> Though I would never read manure-laden pile of toilet paper like Washington Compost, I heard about your Nazi column about "reaching the masses" with your fake news to convince people that your leftist Nazi lies are truth. You are a well-trained serpent of the left, following communist orders as you were taught. "If you say and repeat a lie often enough, it will eventually be seen as truth"—Lenin . . .
>
> Here's what you (slithering, fake-news/propaganda-generating slimy slug) should do: Go fornicate yourself

with a large, sharp knife, and then eat rat poison until your belly is stuffed.

For the first time in my life, I was being called the "*c*-word" on a regular basis. One reader suggested I have my breasts cut off. Again, the misogyny was overwhelming. I wasn't writing about gender issues, but somehow the mere notion that a woman was asserting strong opinions set off the haters in an inexplicable way. I tried to let it roll off my back and even found it amusing when a Trump supporter referred to me as a "venomous serpent," something that my friends told me to treat as a bizarre badge of honor. The *New York Times* reporter John Schwartz, one of the kindest and funniest people I got to know during my time as public editor, suggested I title my memoir *Memories of a Venomous Serpent*. The humor helped, and for a while I put the description in my Twitter bio with a tiny green snake image. All of this vitriol seemed to have little direct relationship to what I was writing—it mattered only that I was critical of Trump and his right-wing media allies. Of course, my experience was relatively minor compared to that of reporters, including those at the *Post*, who covered Trump on a daily basis. It may have been worst of all for broadcast journalists like NBC's Katy Tur, who covered the 2016 Trump campaign. Trump seemed obsessed with Tur, singling her out for public abuse at rallies or media appearances, calling her "Little Katy" and recommending she be fired for incompetence or dishonesty. Her network eventually had to provide her with a private security detail.

Trump's acceptance speech in Cleveland taunted his enemies in the mainstream media. "If you want to hear the corporate spin, the carefully crafted lies, and the media myths—the Democrats are holding their convention next week. Go there." And, as I wrote in one column from Cleveland, he cast himself as truth-teller-in-chief, all while lying incessantly: "I will tell you the plain facts that have been edited out of your nightly news and your morning newspaper." He lumped Hillary Clinton in with the rest of the establishment, as the very symbol of it: "Big business, elite media and major donors are lining up behind my opponent because they know she will keep our rigged system in place."

At that early point, I was still looking for common ground with the Trump crowd—the kind I had always been able to find with readers of all political stripes. Never during my years at *The Buffalo News* did I believe that I couldn't listen to or communicate with readers, no matter what their party affiliation. And I cultivated that. After I moved into a management position, I made sure that I had no political party affiliation; I was registered to vote as a "blank." So, at first, I sought this same open-minded connection with Trump's fans. At the Cleveland airport, I talked with one convention delegate, a concierge for a car dealership named Mary Sue McCarty, who wore a cowboy hat and pearls as she waited for her flight home to Dallas. She was friendly and personable, but certainly had her mind made up about the news media: "Journalists aren't doing their jobs. They are protecting a certain class." When I pointed out that it was *The New York Times* that broke the story about Hillary Clinton's email misdeeds, and that mainstream media organizations (including

The Washington Post) had aggressively investigated the financial practices of the Clinton Foundation, she shrugged off these facts: "If it's a Republican, it's investigated to death. If it's a Democrat, it's breezed over." McCarty could hardly have been more wrong. The media's endless emphasis on Clinton's email practices doomed her campaign perhaps more than any other factor—though there were many factors to choose from.

Stoking anti-press resentment wasn't new in 2016, of course. In fact, attacks on the press are as old as the United States itself, as the media scholars Michael Socolow and Jennifer Moore have documented. In 1775, New York newspaper publisher and British loyalist James Rivington was hanged in effigy—and nearly tarred and feathered by the Sons of Liberty. And after Ida B. Wells published reports in the 1890s about lynching, a white mob threatened her and destroyed her press. There were many more examples, some of them violent, throughout the eighteenth and nineteenth centuries. But in my four decades in journalism, I'd never seen anything like the fever pitch I first experienced in Cleveland and then for a long time afterward.

The longtime TV journalist Ted Koppel provided some perspective when I interviewed him immediately after the convention. In 1964, Koppel recalled, Barry Goldwater got the Republican presidential nomination in California's Cow Palace, where signs proclaimed, "Don't Trust the Liberal Media." And now he was seeing similar press-bashing words projected on huge screens at the Cleveland convention. In Koppel's words: "It's a fifty-two-year-old meme." But Trump had fomented a new level of intensity and anger. And Koppel observed that what made Trump different from those in the past who attacked the press "is that Trump has no shame—he'll say anything," no matter how demonstrably untrue.

Koppel was right. But, for a long time, members of the mainstream press didn't seem to want to use the word "lie" for Trump's constant barrage of falsehoods. It was a bridge they simply didn't want to cross. Top editors explained their reluctance. To lie, they said, means to intend to be untruthful. Since we journalists couldn't be inside a candidate's or a politician's head, how were we supposed to know if—by this definition—they were really lying? The logic eventually became strained, given that Trump blithely repeated the same rank falsehoods over and over. If that wasn't intentional, what was it?

Reporters and their editors couldn't seem to figure out how to cover Trump properly. They didn't even seem to want to. From the moment he descended the golden escalator at Manhattan's Trump Tower in June 2015 to announce his candidacy for president, the mainstream media was in his thrall. They couldn't stop writing about him, showing his image on TV, and even broadcasting the empty stage waiting for him to arrive and start a rally. Trump had described himself as "the ratings machine," and for once he wasn't exaggerating.

In my columns, I criticized the press's obsession with the former reality-TV star, but I was caught up in it, too. I knew that if I wrote a column about Trump, it would find a passionate audience: thousands of comments, thousands of retweets, hundreds of emails, requests to talk on TV and on the radio. And because I wrote about the news media, and Trump never stopped using the news media as a foil, there was so much to say. Some of it was about Trump's terrible treatment of the press and his willful lack of understanding of its role in democratic society. But I was also appalled by the mainstream press's frequently poor performance and the way it was enabling this utterly unsuitable candidate. Part of the problem was that Trump was such a magnet for audience attention. A month before the 2016 election, I pointed an accusatory finger at the head of a certain cable news network. My column began:

> Looking for someone specific to hold responsible for the improbable rise of Donald Trump? Although there are many options, you could do worse than to take a hard look at Jeff Zucker, president of CNN Worldwide. It was Zucker, after all, who as the new head of NBC Entertainment gave Trump his start in reality TV with "The Apprentice" and then milked the real estate developer's uncanny knack for success for all it was worth in ratings and profits.

It was worth plenty. Trump as reality-TV star had dramatically boosted NBC's ratings and Zucker's career. A decade later, during the Republican primary, Zucker's CNN led the way in giving Trump untold amounts of free airtime and reaped the benefits in soaring ratings and revenue. I concluded with a rhetorical question: "Twice, Zucker made Trump a winner. And twice, Trump made Zucker a winner. But what about the rest of us?"

Of course, CNN was far from alone in using Trump to boost ratings and advertising dollars. Les Moonves was talking about political advertising, goosed by Trump's primary campaign, when early in 2016, according to *The Hollywood Reporter*, he said the quiet part out loud: "It may not be good for America, but it's damn good for CBS. . . . The money's rolling in, and this is fun. It's a terrible thing to say. But, bring it on, Donald. Keep going." Donald Trump was more than happy to oblige.

The worst of the press's performance was the way it sought to normalize Trump's behavior. In every way, Trump was a deeply abnormal candidate, but the news media couldn't seem to communicate that effectively or even grasp the problem. Instead, his every unhinged, middle-of-the-night tweet was covered like legitimate news. Typical enough was the day he apparently woke up and decided to go after General Motors in a tweet ranting about a Mexican-made version of the Chevrolet Cruze being shipped across the border and sold tax-free. It came with his threat: "Make in U.S.A. or pay big border tax!" As GM's stock took a hit, the corporation responded that all the Cruze sedans sold in America were made in Ohio, but the episode made news, and gave Trump another attention boost to feed his insatiable appetite. On those rare occasions when he would read a speech with a veneer of seriousness or stick to a teleprompter script, TV pundits would solemnly forecast that a change was in the wind: Candidate Trump was becoming "presidential." Paradoxically, there was some excellent journalistic digging about Trump. *The Washington Post* produced a full-length book, *Trump Revealed*, in August 2016—months before the election—that detailed the candidate's business failures and described his shady character. But this kind of information didn't seem to make a dent.

The reason was the key to so much of the campaign coverage: *No one really thought Trump would win.*

And so, in the late afternoon of November 8, 2016, election day, I walked into the *Washington Post* newsroom with a column already started about Hillary Clinton's supposedly inevitable victory. A few hours later, I was scrambling, just like every reporter, editor, and commentator across the media. My colleagues and I watched the television screens placed all around the newsroom as one battleground state after another fell to Trump. The Rust Belt states that made up the supposed "blue wall" were tumbling into the Republican column.

Tossing away my useless column about Hillary Clinton, I wrote something quite different: that the media coverage of the 2016 race had been, as I put it, "an epic fail." I accused the mainstream press—college-educated, left-leaning, and coastal—of missing the story of what was going on in most of America. These reporters and editors couldn't believe that the nation they knew (or thought they knew) "could embrace someone who mocked a disabled man, bragged about sexually assaulting women, and spouted misogyny, racism and anti-Semitism." They employed a kind of magical thinking: A Trump presidency *shouldn't* happen, therefore it won't happen. And Trump, who delighted in calling journalists "scum"—or worse—alienated us so much that we couldn't see what was right in front of our eyes.

In that column, which I wrote on deadline with my hands shaking under the stress, I predicted that we in the media had some reckoning to do: "Although eating crow is never appealing, we'll be digesting feathers and beaks in the next weeks and months—and maybe years."

Part of that reckoning had to include acknowledging the way mainstream news organizations had covered the campaign, giving Trump untold amounts of free exposure and vastly overblowing the Clinton email story, making it into a scandal far beyond what it deserved, particularly when the *Times* splashed it all over the front page. And of course, other news organizations took their cues from the *Times.*

After I filed my column sometime before midnight on election day, I stood around with several of my *Post* colleagues, trying to process what had just happened. One editor, a young Black woman, was emotional. For her, the vast empowering of Trump's racism and misogyny that was about to occur when he took office as perhaps the most powerful man in the world amounted to an existential threat. It was hard to know just what this would mean, but she had a strong sense that it wouldn't be good for her, and tears welled in her eyes. Another colleague, an older white editor, tried to provide some perspective and give her a little comfort. He confidently predicted that we were all about to get what every journalist yearns for: "It's going to be a great story." They were both right, as it turned out, and their respective reactions speak volumes about how the coming years would affect Americans in widely varying ways, with media figures too often seeing politics as an entertaining game and a boon to business, but not always focused on the real-world effects, especially on vulnerable citizens.

I didn't get to stand around and talk for very long. Soon, the word filtered down from the boss, Marty Baron, that I should produce a second column before I left the newsroom that night. He wanted me to write my recommendations for how the traditional press should cover Trump in the weeks and months ahead. I hadn't given this a lot of thought previously, since I had been convinced, like most other people, that it would never come to pass. But there was no choice, and a new deadline loomed.

So I wrote a call to arms for American journalists. It started like this: "Journalists are going to have to be better—stronger, more courageous, stiffer-spined—than they've ever been." I filed it, not at all convinced that I'd written anything worthwhile on this momentous night, said goodnight to my editor, and headed out of the newsroom at about 3 A.M. Stunned and spent, I walked slowly through the deserted streets of downtown Washington. As I neared my apartment, only blocks away from the National Mall and the White House, I could see the U.S. Capitol to the east: lit from within, glowing an ethereal white in the darkness.

I slept for only three hours. The next day, I took a look at the thousands of comments on my first column from the night before, and I could see how disgusted the public, or at least the *Washington Post* readership, was with the news media's performance during the campaign. "Tragic stupidity," wrote one. In a reference to the high-speed train, the Acela, that runs between New York City and Washington, the reader criticized "the Acela elites who did not see this coming because no one they know would ever vote for a crude piece of work like Trump." Journalists are supposed to listen, not make assumptions. But in general, they had failed to do that enough or effectively. Other readers complained about the media's normalization of Trump and demonization of Clinton. The readers had it right.

A month after Trump was elected, campaign aides for both sides gathered at the Harvard Kennedy School for a traditional post-election debriefing. A Clinton aide, Robby Mook, tore into the media coverage. The press hadn't covered Clinton's policy positions seriously: "They were treating her as the likely winner and they were constantly trying to unearth secrets and reveal and expose. . . . And then you put on top of that Comey and you put on top of that WikiLeaks." He was alluding to something that had happened late in the campaign: Just after *The Washington Post* broke the story about Trump's bragging to an NBC *Access Hollywood* host about groping women (this briefly looked like a death blow for Trump's campaign), WikiLeaks started tweeting links to emails hacked from the personal account of Clinton aide John Podesta. It set off weeks of embarrassment for Clinton just before election day. "I love WikiLeaks!" Trump gloated at a Pennsylvania campaign rally.

Like sharks to chum, the press fed greedily on the hacked emails, not sufficiently providing context about where they might have come from—as it turned out, a Russian cyber-intrusion into the Democratic National Committee, meant to turn the election to Trump. Mook's analysis, though clearly partisan, was largely correct. Much of the campaign coverage had been not only tone-deaf but unfair. And that was separate from the right-wing media, led by Fox News, which long before election day had become Trump's best friend and gave a powerful boost to his quest.

In the weeks that followed, I wanted some deeper insight into what had happened and why, and what the role of the news media had been. So, in 2017, I made some decisions about travel that might have seemed crazy. I turned down invitations to speak in Moscow, Istanbul, and Paris (the whole world, it seemed, wanted to hear expert insights about what Trump meant for the United States and beyond), and instead traveled to domestic destinations, particularly in red states or those that had flipped red for Trump: Alabama, Arizona, Indiana, and Wisconsin. I resolved to listen more than talk.

Part of my determination to understand came from a hostile email I'd received from a *Washington Post* reader, Daniel Hastings, who wrote to me frequently, though he didn't like my work. He thought I was out of touch with real America. "No one outside your liberal bubble at the *Post* or the general DC area can take you seriously," he charged. And he used a favorite Trumpism to deliver an insult: "Ergo, fake news!" Hastings challenged me to go listen to people with a different viewpoint: "Take a visit to the heart of the country. Go to a diner or a flea market. Strike up some conversations. Come back and report without malice or deceit."

The month after the inauguration, I drove to Luzerne County in Pennsylvania, near Scranton and Wilkes-Barre. I had chosen the location carefully, since it was a place where voting registration was heavily Democratic, where voters had favored Barack Obama in 2008 and 2012, and which had flipped decisively to Trump. It wasn't an exaggeration to say that counties like Luzerne, all over the country, gave Trump the presidency. I wanted to understand people's news habits and their thinking about the new president. I found plenty of people to talk to—among them an army recruiter and a community-college student.

Toward evening, I stopped in at J. J. Banko's Seafood restaurant in West Nanticoke, where neon beer signs glowed and a classic song by The Band, "The Weight," was playing on the jukebox as bar patrons sang along. (The lyric "I pulled into Nazareth, was feelin' about half past dead" is a reference, appropriately enough, to a Pennsylvania town only seventy miles away, not to the biblical city.) I was the only woman in the place other than the bartender. After a few conversations I figured out that this was a heavily pro-Trump crowd, and people here were in particular agreement with his hard-line immigration stance and his America-first trade rhetoric. One man told me he read the local paper; several said they watched Fox News. But most memorable was a bearded and soft-spoken forty-year-old construction worker named Dave Kuniega, who described his news sources as local TV and "whatever pops up on my phone." He had followed the campaign but disliked both candidates, so he went against a lifelong tradition that had been ingrained by his parents, who leaned Democratic—he stayed home on election day.

Trump inspired passion, however misguided. Clinton left many voters cold. I had no doubt that there was a big dose of sexism in the reaction of some, but it didn't change the facts. A lot of potential Democratic voters simply shrugged and abstained, rather than pull the lever for her. (Besides, everyone knew Trump could never win; the media had told them so.)

A few months later, I spent some time in New York State's most Republican congressional district, where I once again buttonholed local people, wanting to understand their news habits and their politics. I stopped at places like Paulette's Blue Collar Inn in Angola, a village near the shore of Lake Erie, and spent a day at the Erie County Fair in the Buffalo suburb of Hamburg. I didn't say this out loud, but I was looking for common ground—the sense that American citizens might have wildly different opinions but that we all understood that there was an agreed-upon basis of reality.

After talking to thirty-five people, I came away discouraged. I thought about Yeats's apocalyptic poem "The Second Coming," with its dire lines: "The best lack all conviction, while the worst / Are full of passionate intensity." Most people I talked to just didn't care much about the news, shrugged off the implications of a Trump presidency, and seemed uninterested in following the news closely or critically, except for those who hated the press. One of these was Jason Carr from Green Bay, Wisconsin, who was visiting his girlfriend in Western New York. He was wearing a "Born to Chill" T-shirt and sitting behind the wheel of his Ford F-150 pickup truck as he told me that the mainstream media is nothing but a "puppet show," one that is "filtered and censored" by big business. He spun out conspiracy theories: The United States government was responsible for the 9/11 attacks. And the 2012 massacre of small children in Newtown, Connecticut, never happened; it was staged, he was convinced.

As for the members of the traditional press—people like me, in other words—Carr scoffed, with real disgust in his voice: "I don't believe anything they say. They get paid to be wrong." I left conversations like this feeling almost sickened. I couldn't help but recognize that when it came to acknowledging basic truths, huge swaths of America were very far gone. As for my longtime belief that, as an independent-minded journalist, I could communicate with almost anyone and that we all shared a common basis of reality? Gone, too.

11

"Fake News," You Say?

One summer day several years after the 2016 election, I introduced myself to a store manager in rural New York State, someone I wanted to interview in this heavily Republican district dotted with pro-Trump signs. After I identified myself as a writer for *The Washington Post,* he responded with a grin and what he probably thought was a devilishly clever quip, "So, fake news, right?" I didn't find it funny, but I eked out a weak smile and got him to talk to me.

How had it happened that a reference to one of America's most prestigious news outlets would bring such a disparaging response? It was far from unusual in my experience. The distrust of the mainstream press seems to get worse every day. Like so many institutions—business, education, the police—the American news media is far less trusted than it used to be. In 2021, a global study by the Reuters Institute put Americans' trust in the media at a rock-bottom 29 percent, the lowest of any of the forty-six countries surveyed. What on earth happened to the United States as a beacon of free expression and democracy?

The country was splintering. You could no longer depend

on your neighbors functioning from the same set of facts as you were. There were many factors at play, but none more glaring than cable TV networks, especially Rupert Murdoch's hyperpartisan Fox News, which stoked its viewers' outrage, night after night. Local newspapers, although relatively well trusted in their communities, were going out of business or were bought by private-equity companies that cut their newsroom staffs to the bone. Opinions, not facts, were what the internet thrived on. Facebook alone was well on its way to being one of the chief enemies of democracy, as its algorithms favored the crazily false over the verifiably factual. People's news feeds were inundated with various posts from organizations and people passing along supposed "news" that was at best skewed and at worse just outright false. In the 2016 election, Facebook became a pawn in Russia's disinformation campaign in the United States; no problem, as long as profits kept soaring.

If I had to answer in two words the question of how we got here, they would come easily enough. Not "Donald Trump," though those might garner second place. The words would be "Fox News." From my observation, there's been no greater influence, and it is a terribly negative one, on America's ability to tell truth from lies, or even to care about the difference. The network is not the only culprit but, because of its wide influence and the number of Americans who see it as their primary, if not sole, news source, it's definitely in first place.

In 2019, the great investigative reporter Jane Mayer wrote a stunning eleven-thousand-word piece in *The New Yorker* called "The Making of the Fox News White House." Through deep reporting, Mayer explored the symbiotic closeness between Donald Trump and the conservative cable network, and strongly suggested that Fox had moved beyond mere partisanship to straight-out propaganda. It had become something close to state television. Her investigation was masterfully done, and it resonated widely. Everyone knew, of course, how much Trump had benefitted from the conservative network's support, but this piece nailed down how it had happened and what effect Fox was having on American society. Within days, Democratic National Committee chairman Tom Perez announced that Fox News would no longer be considered as one of the hosts of the upcoming Democratic primary debates. That decision set off right-wing howls of censorship, though it struck me as a reasonable business decision based on the latest information. Why play ball with your mortal enemy?

When I read Mayer's article, I was already well versed in Fox's methods. I had been the media columnist for *The Washington Post* for nearly three years, and Trump had been the president for almost all of this period. I had written many columns about the network. I was harshly critical of how it had misled its viewers about the death of Seth Rich, a twenty-seven-year-old staffer for the Democratic National Committee, who in the summer of 2016 was fatally shot in the back on a Washington street. Based on some dubious reporting from his own network, Fox's prime-time star Sean Hannity relentlessly spun the notion that this might well be an inside job by the DNC—retribution by Hillary Clinton's camp for Rich's supposed sharing of emails with WikiLeaks. In other words, Hannity came close to suggesting that Hillary or her people had ordered Seth Rich killed. This conspiracy-mongering was nonsense, and it was cruel to Rich's family, who first protested the coverage and then filed suit against the network. Meanwhile, the police had concluded Rich probably was the victim of a robbery gone sideways.

As a columnist, I had many other occasions to look askance at Fox's coverage and commentary. The network tried to present itself as "fair and balanced," but it often was nothing of the sort, and never intended to be. Fox was founded to fulfill its founders' vision to make oodles of profit by fostering conservative outrage, as addictively as possible.

Impressed by the scope and detail of Jane Mayer's reporting, I decided to take my writing a step further. I thought it was important to build on Mayer's work and raise awareness about how Fox News functioned, almost as an arm of the Trump administration. So I took a big swing in a column titled "It's Time—High Time—to Take Fox News's Destructive Role in America Seriously." Everyone ought to see Fox for what it is, I wrote. It shouldn't be treated as a normal news organization with mistakes, flaws, and commercial concerns that may get in the way of serving the public interest. It was something quite different: a shameless propaganda outfit, making billions each year even as it attacks core democratic values such as tolerance, truth, and fair elections. In addition to serving as a megaphone for the right, I noted, Fox rarely corrected or acknowledged its own errors, which is one hallmark of legitimate news organizations. (It did retract the Seth Rich reporting, but it took Hannity too long to stop his on-air disinformation campaign; the family's suit resulted in a settlement.)

I pointed out that Fox doesn't have the kind of ethics and standards department that most networks have, and it certainly doesn't make its news standards public, as many outlets do. However, since the network enjoys First Amendment protections for the most part, it can broadcast what it wants, no matter how many falsehoods are spread as a result. I noted that there were some legitimate news people at Fox, including Chris Wallace, Bret Baier, and Shepard Smith. (Smith later left the network; he told Christiane Amanpour that he couldn't countenance staying any longer because of all the lies disseminated on the Fox opinion shows. By late 2021, Wallace had left the network, too, headed for CNN's new streaming service.) I concluded with this line: "Despite the skills of a few journalists who should have long ago left the network in protest, Fox News has become an American plague." I was certainly pushing the limits of my role as a news-side columnist providing "perspective," as my column was labeled, but I heard no complaints from the *Post* brass. I was confident that Marty Baron—while he didn't always agree with me—supported my right to call things as I saw them.

The "Fox is an American plague" column went viral. It sped to the top of the most-read stories on the *Post* site that day and stayed there for a long time, attracting hundreds of thousands of readers. It found thousands more on social media. More than five thousand commenters added their thoughts on the *Post* site. One of them expressed the core problem well, and with considerable reserve: "It is a relief to see this brought out into the light of day, as I truly believe Fox 'News' to be a key force in undermining the fabric of our society, and a grave threat to our well-being. But in a nation that cherishes free speech, rightfully, the most effective response to such a scourge remains elusive." One of my editors, David Malitz, would later refer to this piece as my "Fox-is-the-actual-devil column."

If I'd had few friends at Fox before, I had none now. Even before this I knew that anything I wrote about the network would be picked apart by its aggressive public relations staff, searching for any mistake, no matter how inconsequential, that they could bring to my editors' attention. I had the sense that they were hoping to embarrass me by getting a correction appended to my column and that this kind of potential misery might give me pause before writing another such piece. I did write about Fox again and again, always trying to make my columns especially bulletproof.

All of this was uncomfortable. I was used to criticism, but the tone and level of vitriol had reached new highs, as I received nasty responses from right-wing readers who threatened and insulted me by email and voicemail. The security staff at the *Post* tried to determine if the writers were just nasty or whether they might actually be dangerous. Often these messages contained the worst kind of profanity and misogyny. Even the relatively mild missives began to disturb my peace of mind because they arrived in such volume. "It sickens me that people like you post lies and deception to the public," wrote one *Post* reader to me. "This article has no right to be printed to the public. You are what is wrong with this country. Shame on you!" Despite the downside, I didn't think I should stop. I knew all too well that Fox was doing harm, and, I figured, what was the point of having my bully pulpit as *Post* media columnist if I didn't try to bring such things to light?

Let's take a deeper look at the term "fake news." It was not really in use until late 2014 (when BuzzFeed's Craig Silverman started using it to describe published lies he was investigating), but it would come to define much of the problem. It had a double meaning: one literal and one more diabolical. Fake news could mean intentional lies dressed up to look like legitimate news stories that spread on social media like oil slicks. It was *that* kind of fake news that convinced millions of people, during the 2016 presidential campaign, that Pope Francis had endorsed Donald Trump's presidential bid or that Hillary Clinton was running a child sex ring out of a Washington, D.C., pizza joint. But then there were the cynical cries of "fake news" from politicians—with Trump leading the way—that really meant "this is a story I don't like." Trump famously told CBS News's Lesley Stahl that he disparaged the press purposefully: "I do it to discredit you all and demean you all, so when you write negative stories about me no one will believe you." Appallingly, it worked.

Another part of the problem was that traditional news organizations, "Big Journalism," didn't know how to handle this shifting ground. Should they call out the lies? Should they bend over backward to normalize political behavior that was blasting through every guardrail of democracy? Should they try to look even-handed and neutral at any cost, giving equal treatment to both sides of a political conflict, even if the two sides aren't equally valid? They didn't seem to know. And too often, they seemed to be in a defensive crouch, while right-wing commentators branded them as left-wing activists.

The metastasizing lies from Trump and his media allies became an inevitable theme of my columns. Every day brought fresh evidence that truth was roadkill for the new president and his surrogates. Some days were more vivid than others. One of these came in late 2016, a few weeks after the election, when I was a guest on Diane Rehm's syndicated radio show. I was in the studio at WAMU, the public radio station in Washington, sitting next to James Fallows, the respected *Atlantic* writer and former White House speechwriter, and Glenn Thrush, then at Politico. We all listened, wide-eyed, as Rehm interviewed a guest who had joined us remotely, Scottie Nell Hughes, a frequent media surrogate for Trump. The conversation spanned subjects from flag burning to Trump's evidence-free assertion that he, not Hillary Clinton, would have won the popular vote if millions of immigrants had not voted illegally. With remarkable directness, Hughes fended off Rehm's suggestions that there was a real problem with Trump's habitual lying.

"There's no such thing, unfortunately, anymore, [as] facts," she memorably declared at one point. Hughes, who had been a paid commentator for CNN during the campaign, kept defending that assertion and her own qualification as what she called a "classically studied journalist." None of us knew quite what that meant.

Truth, it was becoming clear, was of no particular concern to the new president. He ordered his press secretary, Sean

Spicer, to lie about the size of the inaugural crowd during the very first press conference of the new administration. It was a bad sign of things to come. "This was the largest audience to ever witness an inauguration—period—both in person and around the globe," Spicer, who had been a Republican National Committee communications director, told reporters just one day after Trump took the oath of office. *The Washington Post*'s Glenn Kessler gave this claim the worst grade, Four Pinocchios, in the "Fact Checker" column. He characterized the briefing as "an appalling performance by the new press secretary." Kessler also observed that Spicer managed to make a series of false and misleading claims in service of a relatively minor issue, rather than pushing back against the president's demands. "Part of a flack's job is to tell the boss when lies are necessary—and when they are not," he wrote.

But Trump's staff was not about to make such distinctions. Ari Fleischer, a former George W. Bush press secretary, characterized the Spicer performance from a position of experience, calling it "a statement you're told to make by the President. And you know the President is watching." MSNBC's Mika Brzezinski referred to it in more vivid terms as "Sean Spicer's first hostage video."

Then it got worse. Trump advisor Kellyanne Conway defended her colleague on *Meet the Press*. Spicer, she said, had been providing "alternative facts" to counter what the media had reported. It was a phrase that would live in infamy. I argued at the time that this should mean that "access journalism," taking official pronouncements at face value for the purpose of scoops, should be declared dead. Only real digging—investigative journalism, in other words—would provide value for the public now. "Spicer's statement should be seen for what it is: Remarks made over the casket at the funeral of access journalism," I wrote, but it would turn out to be nothing but wishful thinking. Access journalism was alive and well during the Trump administration. Reporters continued to seek and amplify whatever the White House had to say, often under the cover of anonymity. In time, letting Trump be Trump would prove not only unwise and undemocratic but actually deadly. A pandemic was on its way, and the president would be in full denial mode. Much of the mainstream media, by now fully in thrall to the president, would be along for the ride.

Of course, Fox News was far from the only media friend of the Trump administration, though it may have been the most influential. But there were others. Infowars, a home for dangerous conspiracy theories, even got a temporary credential to attend White House press briefings at one point. This was the same outfit where Alex Jones—the screaming radio host who founded it—had promulgated disgusting lies. He told his listeners things I'd heard when I talked to ordinary people about their beliefs and their media habits: that 9/11 might well have been planned and executed by the U.S. government, that he doubted that Barack Obama was an American citizen, and that the 2012 massacre of schoolchildren in Newtown, Connecticut, may have been a hoax performed by actors. Under pressure, Jones sometimes recanted: In 2019, during a deposition as part of a defamation suit brought by the Newtown victims' families, he blamed "a form of psychosis" for his belief that the massacre had been staged. But the falsehoods had already taken root for some members of the public.

Watching Fox News function as Trump's amplification system and best friend, I couldn't help but think back to my interest in Watergate, which had drawn me into journalism as a teenager. I had never heard of Roger Ailes back then, but he was already an influence on Richard Nixon, whose presidential run in 1960 had crashed after he compared poorly in televised debate with the more telegenic and charismatic John F. Kennedy. Ailes and Nixon met in 1967, and not long after, Nixon hired him as a consultant with an emphasis on television appearances. That partnership helped Nixon win the presidency for the first time in 1968.

Nixon, of course, would flame out after Watergate, but Ailes only grew more and more influential. He advised Ronald Reagan and George H. W. Bush, helping them get elected with ideas like the "orchestra pit" theory of political campaigning, quipping about the virtues of sensationalism during a run for office: "If you have two guys on a stage and one guy says, 'I have a solution to the Middle East problem,' and the other guy falls in the orchestra pit, who do you think is going to be on the evening news?" If you want to win the news cycle, in other words, create a diversion, a sensation, or an outrage.

By the time Donald Trump was elected, this would all be terribly familiar. Ailes took everything he had learned into his partnership with Rupert Murdoch, the Australian-born media mogul. As David Greenberg, the historian and author of *Republic of Spin: An Inside History of the American Presi-*

dency, wrote in a *New York Times* piece shortly after Ailes died, the media mogul's techniques and philosophy were forged in the Nixon era. Just as Ailes helped Nixon with his television image, the media mogul learned a few things from the thirty-seventh president. "The welter of crimes and abuses of power known as Watergate obviously remains [Nixon's] greatest legacy, as current events are again reminding us," Greenberg wrote. "But in second place would surely be his reshaping of the Republican Party to enshrine his brand of cultural populism as both doctrine and strategy." That couldn't have been done without Ailes and Murdoch, who founded Fox News together in 1996. The entwined roots run deep, and they could hardly be more influential. Like Nixon, Ailes, too, would resign in disgrace, though he lasted much longer. After Fox's parent company settled Gretchen Carlson's sexual harassment case against Ailes for $20 million, the co-founder left the network in 2016 and died the next year. Unfortunately, his legacy lives on.

The paradox of Trump's rise was how much of it he owed to the very media he loved to criticize—both the highly partisan right-wing outlets (he was seldom completely satisfied with their sycophancy) and the mainstream press. He should have sent them thank-you notes for the free advertising instead of blasting them with criticism. During the 2016 campaign CNN gave Trump endless "unearned media" by broadcasting his rallies and speeches live. Why? Because he reliably drew an audience and CNN's top boss, Jeff Zucker, knew that very well. But it wasn't only the cable networks or the extreme partisan sites like Breitbart who were obsessed with Trump. Even those of us at serious outlets like *The Washington Post* came to understand very well that putting Trump's name in a headline would attract readers. It was audience-enhancing magic at a time when news organizations were fighting hard for that big digital audience, tracked in real time on huge screens set up in newsrooms. To varying degrees, many in the overall media world were guilty of playing the "outrage for clicks" game. The more responsible insisted on staying within the realm of truth; others didn't seem to care about that.

One regrettable episode—no friend to mainstream media's reputation for truth-telling—came with the publication by BuzzFeed of the so-called Steele Dossier. It was, in essence, a collection of unprovable allegations dressed up as an intelligence report from a former British intelligence officer meant to damage Donald Trump.

To some on the left, and in left-leaning media, this was manna from heaven. Its most outrageous suggestions about Trump's behavior and connections, though unverifiable, were taken as evidence and gospel. Trump, of course, was all over it, using his Twitter account to brand the dossier "fake news" and to identify a political witch hunt. He wasn't entirely wrong. Its publication and the over-the-top nonsense that followed were a dark chapter for the mainstream press. I wrote about it in my *Post* column, criticizing BuzzFeed's decision to publish it. In an era when trust in the media was already in the gutter, this did absolutely nothing to help. But even that isn't the core point, I wrote, which is far simpler: It's never been acceptable to publish rumor and innuendo.

After several years, when most of the dossier was proven to be meritless, the whole episode became even more regrettable. It was used as a way to "prove" that all the talk about Russia's efforts to influence the 2016 election was also false. That the *Times* and the *Post* should give back their Pulitzer Prizes, won for digging into those connections. That Trump's endless talk about the "Russia hoax" perpetrated by the media was true. That was absurd. Anyone who bothered to read the report issued by special counsel Robert Mueller would know that Russia was guilty of illegal interference "in sweeping and systematic fashion," and that the Trump campaign was willing to receive the help. That the head of the Trump campaign, Paul Manafort, was so involved with Russian operatives that he represented a "grave counterintelligence threat" to the United States. That many of the connections were far beyond inappropriate.

But the overhyping of the dossier's "findings" meant that all of this truth was disparaged. And more broadly, cable news had given far too much attention to speculation about Trump's Russia connections and what the Mueller report might eventually say. A Harmony Labs study published in *Columbia Journalism Review* showed that from election day in 2016 to April 2019, all the cable networks (even Fox, to a lesser extent) became obsessed with the subject, with MSNBC giving 32 percent of its prime-time coverage to the Russia-Trump story. Anyone who watched Rachel Maddow's show might think that number was actually low. "Cable news channels systematically favored the Trump-Russia collusion scandal for nearly three years, clogging the information pipeline citizens depend on to ground their civic participation," the 2019 article noted.

Beyond depriving citizens of a wider spectrum of news, this overkill contributed to an environment in which nuance had no place. And so the cries of "fake news" merely gained traction. All of this was a failure of the reality-based press, and a consequential one.

Still, the damage that the right-wing media was doing was in a class by itself. By undermining reality and spreading misinformation, it was wreaking havoc on American politics and culture. Among Fox News's worst sins over the years: the "birtherism" conspiracy theory that spread the racist falsehood that Barack Obama was not born in the United States and therefore could not be a legitimate president. The hateful depiction of immigrants and refugees at America's southern border, especially the so-called caravan that was making its way through Mexico. The deadly lies downplaying the virus in the early weeks and months of the coronavirus pandemic. The disinformation about rampant fraud in the 2020 presidential election.

January 6, 2021, brought it all home. As I wrote the following day, it was clear to me that the mob that stormed and desecrated the Capitol could not have existed in a country that hadn't been radicalized by the "news" they consumed, day after day, and the spinning of that news by the likes of Hannity,

Tucker Carlson, and Laura Ingraham—the prime-time stars of Fox News.

I almost felt sorry for some of the rioters because they so clearly were the victims of a poisoned media system. I always paid particular attention to the Buffalo angle of any major news story. (Oddly, there almost always *was* such an angle; in Buffalo, we called it the Ann Odre Syndrome, after the local woman, a tourist at the Vatican, who was hit by a stray bullet in 1981 when Pope John Paul II was shot in St. Peter's Square.) So I noted with interest the comments of Jul Thompson, a right-wing activist who boarded one of the two buses traveling from Western New York to Washington for the rally, then gave an interview to *The Buffalo News* about being "absolutely justified" in urging on those who scaled a wall of the Capitol.

After all, Thompson claimed, there had been rampant fraud resulting in a stolen election. "We would like all the courts to see the evidence of massive fraud and election interference," she said. "If they saw the evidence they would have no choice but to rule for Trump." It didn't matter to her, or perhaps she didn't know, that these allegations had already been duly considered by the courts and by election officials, including Republicans, and had been thoroughly rejected. But if your news source was Trump's Twitter feed and Fox News, you might never come across these facts.

Sean Hannity certainly was doing his part on his prime-time Fox show to push the idea of rampant fraud. "I can factually tell you tonight," he informed his audience of millions shortly after the election, "it will be impossible to ever know the true, fair, accurate election results."

The constant misleading of the TV audience was a classic case of Trump projecting his own faults on his enemies. For years, even as he led the political leagues in lying, he charged the mainstream news media with misleading the public. "Fake news!" he cried whenever there was coverage he didn't like because it put him in a bad light.

"The speed with which the term became polarized and in fact a rhetorical weapon illustrates how efficient the conservative media machine has become," said the journalism scholar Nikki Usher when I interviewed her for a column in which I proposed retiring the term. I thought it was unwise to feed the beast of misinformation by adopting Trump's language. Clearly, there is such a thing as false news, meaning actual misinformation in the form of news stories. There are whole industries set up to do it. But the term "fake news" had become so tainted that using it did more harm than good.

It had crept—no, sped—into the lexicon of conservative politicians in a heartbeat. Examples abounded. "You can put all that under the category of fake news," charged Jim DeMint, the former senator and Tea Party member, when he wanted to disparage a TV interviewer's suggestions that Obamacare had merits as well as flaws. "Fake news," blasted the conspiracy theorist Alex Jones when he wanted to deny a news report that Trump's daughter Ivanka would occupy the East Wing offices traditionally reserved for the president's wife. When a right-wing website needed a putdown for ABC News's chief White House correspondent, Jonathan Karl, it called him a "fake-news propagandist." All of this had a clear purpose: shoot the messenger. The phrase quickly moved from the national to the local level, with small-town school board members crying "fake news" in order to delegitimize reporters from local TV stations or weekly newspapers trying to do their jobs.

Trump had a special gift for this kind of memorable language. It was easy to understand, easy to embrace, easy to remember. At the same time, Trump had nicknames for his least favorite news organizations, among them the "Failing *New York Times*" (even as the company's revenue and subscriptions soared to new heights) and the "Amazon *Washington Post*," an unsubtle reference to the paper's owner, Jeff Bezos, another nemesis. (Amazon, which Bezos founded and where he is executive chairman, doesn't own the *Post*.) Misleading, yes—lies, even—but these nicknames tended to stick.

As Trump's second impeachment trial got under way in February 2021, the issue of lies, "alternative facts," and truth came to the forefront immediately. "Democracy needs a ground to stand upon—and that ground is the truth," the lead House impeachment manager, Jamie Raskin, a Maryland Democrat, said in his opening statement, quoting his father, the political activist Marcus Raskin. Raskin, who led the prosecuting team trying to make the case that the forty-fifth president had incited the January 6 attack on the Capitol, urged that the Senate trial not be seen as about lawyers or political parties. No, the trial should be "a moment of truth for America."

Listening to Raskin, I had to wonder: Did truth matter

anymore? Would most Americans know it when they saw it, or would they turn away? How could anyone, I wondered, watch the opening presentation of that trial—particularly the stunning thirteen-minute video that assembled all the pieces of what had happened into a compelling and horrifying chronological narrative—and not acknowledge the importance of the truth? I wrote about the January 6 video footage, saying that it defied the thermodynamic law of the internet age—growing *more* compelling with time, not fading with repetition. How could it be denied? I got my answer: Some Republican senators who would be voting to convict or acquit literally looked away. Rand Paul was doodling on a pad of paper and Rick Scott was busying himself with paperwork, the *Post* reported. Tom Cotton and Marco Rubio, at various points, also turned away from what was on the screen: the truth that Congress had been attacked by a mob inflamed by the president of the United States.

All of this resonated throughout the impeachment trial that resulted in Trump's second acquittal, despite bipartisan support for his conviction; the 57–43 vote fell ten votes short of the two-thirds majority required by the Constitution. The questions remain, but I'm increasingly apprehensive about the answers. One thing I do feel certain of is what that rural store manager would have to say and exactly what phrase he would choose to say it.

The ugliness deepened. In late 2021, Fox News's chief propagandist, Tucker Carlson, put out what he called a documentary about January 6, called "Patriot Purge." It promoted a series of dangerous lies: That the insurrection had been brought about by left-wing agitators, not Trump supporters.

That it was orchestrated inside the government so that these Trump supporters could be persecuted by federal law enforcement. That the left is relentlessly targeting and persecuting "legacy Americans," which is coded language for white people. Shortly after it came out, two high-profile resignations from Fox News followed. Jonah Goldberg and Stephen Hayes, conservative commentators who had told the truth about Trump over the years, called "Patriot Purge" the final straw in their disillusionment. In a resignation post, they called it "a collection of incoherent conspiracy-mongering, riddled with factual inaccuracies, half-truths, deceptive imagery, and damning omissions." They said that it wasn't an isolated incident but "merely the most egregious example of a longstanding trend" which creates "an alternative history of January 6th, contradicted not just by common sense, not just by the testimony and on the record statements of many participants, but by the reporting of the news division of Fox News itself." Goldberg and Hayes removed themselves; they didn't want to be associated with this anymore. But the damage lives on and grows worse.

12

Objectivity Wars and the "Woke" Newsroom

Around the time Marty Baron retired as executive editor of *The Washington Post* in 2021, some famous words of his joined the many inspirational quotations displayed on the walls of the newsroom he had run for eight years, leading the paper to a slew of Pulitzer Prizes. The quote read: "We're not at war . . . we're at work." To those of us who had been in the *Post* newsroom during the Trump administration, this needed no explanation. From editorial clerks to the highest-ranking editors, we all understood what this meant. The words were a kind of shorthand for the *Post's* guiding principle during the tumultuous past five years as Donald Trump dominated the national conversation and headlines. To outsiders or non-journalists, though, they might have seemed cryptic.

The words came from an onstage interview with Baron during a media conference in California about a year into Trump's presidency. They were a response to Trump's portrayal of journalists as his enemy, and as scum and the lowest form of life. He had said he was in a "running war" with the media. His advisor Steve Bannon had been even more inflammatory in an interview with *The New York Times:* "The media here is the opposition party. They don't understand this country. They still do not understand why Donald Trump is the president of the United States." Bannon went even further: "The media should be embarrassed and humiliated and keep its mouth shut and just listen for a while." These were fighting words. And they were meant to be; Bannon knew exactly how maddening they would seem to members of a profession that sees itself as doing a crucial service for the public.

Baron firmly rejected the "opposition party" idea. The fuller form of what he said went like this: "The way I view it is, we're not at war with the administration, we're at work. We're doing our jobs." His paper's journalists were covering Trump not with animosity but with journalistic rigor and independence—the same way, in fact, that they would cover any administration, and the same way they would have covered Hillary Clinton had she been elected. Baron's words were widely quoted and largely agreed with by journalists, and they played well with the public. But for some critics, they came to stand for something else: a view of old-style objectivity that was out of date.

Some thought that the press was wrong not to fight back, wrong to stay with past practice and scrupulously avoid any suggestion of subjectivity. How could journalists keep doing things the tried-and-true way when the president himself was so deeply abnormal, so disrespectful of the basics of how a democracy is supposed to function—including the role of the press?

Was Marty Baron out of sync with the times? He was dubbed "stubbornly retro" by the conservative *National Journal,* and a headline in *The Guardian* picked up on a description of him by *Times* media columnist Ben Smith as the "ultimate old-school editor." He certainly wasn't old-school in dealing with the realities of publishing in the digital era. Baron was skilled in moving the paper forward. By the time he retired, the Post had three million digital subscribers, was solidly profitable, largely due to that growth, and was hiring steadily, as well as opening bureaus all over the world. If this was old-school behavior, it was the kind that many other news executives would like to emulate, just as they would love to claim even a fraction of the ten Pulitzer Prizes the *Post* won during Baron's tenure. Was it, though, an accurate judgment on his journalism ideas? A judgment on "we're not at war . . . we're at work"? To put it bluntly: Is traditional objectivity in need of an update?

In the American press, objectivity has its roots in an effort to counter the irresponsible "yellow journalism" prevalent at the turn of the twentieth century. Beginning around 1920, the renowned writer and reporter Walter Lippmann promoted the idea that reporting should be based on verification and the examination of evidence. This more scientific approach would produce credible journalism very different from the sensationalized crime reporting of the earlier era with its "scare" headlines meant to inflame the public. It was a vast improvement.

Baron, in a 2019 speech, made it clear that while he believes in "objective" journalism and has no problem with using that adjective, it's not about false equivalency. It's about approaching every subject with an open mind, rigorously reporting without bias, and then telling the truth, as gleaned, in a straightforward manner. Just as we expect a judge or a police officer to put their own feelings aside when doing their jobs, so, too, should a journalist. That's objectivity, in his view.

This is not "on-the-one-hand, on-the-other-hand journalism as it is often wrongly defined," Baron said. It involves thorough, meticulous, fair-minded research and the clear relating to the public of what was discovered.

The "war/work" expression, though, had spurred debate. It became such an iconic sentence that New York University professor Jay Rosen, one of the nation's preeminent press critics, wrote a long thread about it on Twitter and mentioned it in a lengthy piece in *The New York Review of Books*. He viewed it as "genius"—but genius with some troubling limits built into it. First, he gave the phrase due credit. "Hard to overstate how seductive 'just do your job' is," Rosen wrote. "It combines the myth of taciturn manliness (Gary Cooper) with the appeal of the humble public servant (I'm no hero, ma'am, just doin' my job)."

Rosen then introduced his concerns: "To say 'we're not at war; we're at work' does not speak to the enormity of the problem. Somehow the press has to figure out how to fight back." You don't fight back effectively, he suggested, by staying with past practice even when it is time-honored. Somehow, he wrote, journalists actually *do* have to go to war against a political style embodied by Trump "in which power gets to write its own story."

Is there such a thing as objectivity and is it worth striving for? The inside-journalism fight about objectivity—which deals with questions like these—has been raging for decades. I wrote about one aspect of it at the *Times* when I considered the notion of "false balance" or "false equivalency" and rejected the ingrained journalistic practice of giving equal weight to both sides of an argument.

This debate intensified in the Trump era. In the aftermath of the 2020 election, followed by Trump's second impeachment for inciting the deadly riot at the Capitol on January 6, 2021, it ramped up even more.

To some observers, and some journalists, it seemed like traditional news coverage wasn't getting the job done in an era when there was so much bad-faith behavior. Wasn't it time to call out political misbehavior more forcefully? Wasn't it time to call a lie a lie? To use "racist" instead of "racially tinged"? Didn't we owe it to the public to emphasize *true* fairness over performative neutrality?

Wherever I traveled in recent years, whether on assignment or not, I always made a point to talk to people about where they got their news and what they liked and didn't like about the news media. I'd often hear that they wanted less opinion—less spin, as they saw it. They would say something like: "Just give me the facts and let me make up my own mind." I heard over and over that journalists should keep their own point of view out of their work, and that people were disgusted by what they called the "bickering" they saw on cable news.

They seemed to be seeking what Rosen called "the view from nowhere." Rosen opposed this; if objectivity is defined as having no point of view, then objectivity is impossible and not even worth striving for. Instead, he approvingly echoed a line from the author David Weinberger: "Transparency is the new objectivity." Declare your biases up front, and let the reader or viewer understand where you are coming from.

Rosen went further still. The old ways were *hurting* the cause of truth seeking, which is what journalism is supposed to be about. Everybody has beliefs and prejudices, and everybody has a point of view, Rosen said, so why not be honest about it? And others made the point that the media often presented "objective" reality from an outdated point of view: one based on society's white, male hierarchy.

On his blog in 2021, Rosen made a detailed case for journalists to be transparent with their audiences or readership about what they believe. For context, he harkened back to the longtime CBS News anchorman Walter Cronkite, whose famous sign-off was "And that's the way it is." This omniscient neutrality is one way to make a bid for trust. But a different way, perhaps better suited to this moment, is to say, in essence, "You can trust my reporting because I put myself into it, and I'm telling you who I am." Rosen gave examples of how this might work. The well-respected investigative journalism outlet ProPublica tells readers that it practices a particular kind of journalism, the point of which is "to expose abuses of power and betrayals of the public trust by government, business, and other institutions." Rosen calls this a disclosure of intent, one that is nonpartisan, neither red nor blue. He wrote:

> If the powerful cannot be held accountable, democracy becomes a joke. Abuses of the public trust are a special category of wrongs to be righted. In journalism the point of investigating is not just to document wrongdoing but to get results. That—in my paraphrase—is where *ProPublica* is coming from: "Using the moral force of investigative journalism to spur reform through the sustained spotlighting of wrongdoing," as they put it.

Another example of this transparency, from the right-leaning website The Dispatch, does have a political stance and is clear about it: "We don't apologize for our conservatism. Some of the best journalism is done when the author is honest with readers about where he or she is coming from, and some of the very worst journalism hides behind a pretense of objectivity and the stolen authority that pretense provides."

Can these points of view be reconciled? I don't think Marty Baron and Jay Rosen are as far apart as one might think. While not in perfect sync, they don't really represent two ends of a continuum, even though Baron says he's in favor of old-fashioned objectivity and Rosen rejects that. But both believe in truth, and in good journalism as a bulwark of democracy. It's a difference in approach and in language.

I agree with the notion that more transparency would actually give journalists more credibility than pretending to be completely without viewpoint or, worse, presenting both sides of a given political controversy as equal. Too often, the allegiance to objectivity ends up with an unintended consequence, a kind of defensive neutrality sometimes described as "both-sides" journalism, in which unequal claims are treated as if they were equally valid. That's no good. To put it in simple terms: If one side claims it's raining outside, and the other side claims the sun is shining, it's not journalists' job to quote both equally; it's their job to walk outside, look at the sky, and report the truth.

Two think-tank scholars, Norman Ornstein and Thomas Mann, expressed the problem with "both-sides-equal" journalism beautifully in a 2012 opinion piece for *The Washington Post.* The italics are mine: "We understand the values of mainstream journalists, including the effort to report both sides of a story. *But a balanced treatment of an unbalanced phenomenon distorts reality.* If the political dynamics of Washington are unlikely to change any time soon, at least we should change the way that reality is portrayed to the public."

That makes sense. But for those who want to pass off a lie as truth—like that the 2020 election was stolen from Donald Trump through a rigged voting system—any reform of the old way is something to be fought off. Why? Because they want equal time to spout the lie. And in recent years they successfully made the case that they should get it. They often did, on the Sunday TV talk shows, on cable news panels of pundits, and in the columns of America's most prestigious newspapers, where "conservative" writers—sometimes misrepresenting reality—were hired to show how very nonpartisan the papers were.

Some journalists, though, were able to cut through all of that nonsense. One was Maria Ressa, the brilliant and admirable journalist who was persecuted relentlessly for her reporting on the autocratic Duterte administration in her country, the Philippines, and who won the Nobel Peace Prize in 2021. After the award was announced, her views on the subject were revisited and celebrated. "In a battle for facts, in a battle for truth, journalism is activism," she had told National Public Radio the previous year.

As she said in her Nobel Prize acceptance speech, talking about the social media platforms, particularly Facebook:

> These American companies controlling our global information ecosystem are biased against facts, biased against journalists. They are—by design—dividing us and radicalizing us.
>
> Without facts, you can't have truth. Without truth, you can't have trust. Without trust, we have no shared reality, no democracy, and it becomes impossible to deal with our world's existential problems: climate, coronavirus, the battle for truth.

I explored these subjects—truth, trust, and objectivity—over and over again at the *Post,* and in the process I figured out my own stance. Although I had come of age at a time when "the view from nowhere" was practiced religiously, my position became more and more like Ressa's.

Journalism, practiced in a democratic crisis, *is* a form of activism. How else to deal with the way the 2020 election and the January 6 insurrection at the Capitol were being lied about by Trump and by the Republicans, with whom he still held so much influence? Washington journalists were often guilty of taking things down the middle in exactly the way Ornstein and Mann had warned. In one column, I put the problem this way: "Mainstream journalists want their work to be perceived as fair-minded and non-partisan. They want to defend themselves against charges of bias. So they equalize the unequal. This practice seems so ingrained as to be unresolvable."

There were journalists, including on TV, who were able to take a constructive approach. On CNN, Jake Tapper made a decision not to have any members of the so-called insurrection caucus on his Sunday show, *State of the Union*. Why, he reasoned, should they be given the opportunity to spread their lies in the name of fairness? Others who didn't have Tapper's decision-making leeway found themselves frustrated by the old ways.

I interviewed Andrew Taylor, a well-respected and longtime reporter for the Associated Press, which prides itself on its impartiality and usually delivers the news in a direct "just the facts" way, with no opinion creeping in. In the minds of many news professionals and news consumers, the AP is the quintessential objective news organization: It plays everything straight. Taylor did it that way for a long time and developed a reputation as one of the most knowledgeable reporters covering Congress. But he was growing disillusioned with the way, in his words, politics had started going off the rails, particularly with the ascendancy of the Tea Party movement—the conservative Republicans who made it their business to oppose everything President Obama tried to get done. Then came January 6.

Taylor was at his desk in the Daily Press Gallery within the Capitol building on that day, and when the Senate abruptly stopped its session as rioters entered the building, he was one of those who huddled inside the chamber while the violence and chaos raged. He was physically unhurt but profoundly affected on a mental and emotional level, telling me he found himself angry and agitated in the weeks that followed. In the spring of 2021, he quit the AP. Part of the reason, he told me, was that he had become concerned about the kind of reporting he and his colleagues had been doing for many years; he had come to believe that it was no longer capable of really transmitting the full truth given how much dishonesty and political posturing he observed among members of Congress. He was particularly critical of House minority leader Kevin McCarthy, the California Republican and Trump loyalist, referring to him as among the worst of those lawmakers whose "approach to their jobs is too often bad-faith bullshit."

After decades in the business (Taylor began his career clipping news articles for reporters at *Congressional Quarterly* in the 1980s), he was done with daily news reporting. Part of the reason was how deeply he was affected by the trauma of January 6. Part of it was disillusionment.

"The rules of objective journalism require you to present facts to tell a true story, but the objective-journalism version of events can often obscure the reality of what's really going on," he told me. He was blunt about the unfortunate results: "It sanitizes things." Maybe objective-style journalism used to be an adequate way to cover Washington politics and government, he said—but no longer. Taylor's sentiments, which resonated deeply with many who read my column about him, probably couldn't have been uttered while he was still working for a mainstream news organization. To question the notion of objectivity is to open yourself up to charges of bias, of slanting the news to reflect your own politics. And so mainstream news organizations practice it—or they say they do. They don't stop to question whether they are, in Taylor's words, obscuring reality by presenting everything in a neutral way that normalizes the abnormal.

After I wrote about Taylor, I heard from Marty Baron, who had recently retired. He told me that what Taylor was describing wasn't objectivity at all. I followed up with him in person and by email to understand his point of view more fully. He wrote:

> Journalists use the word "objectivity" in all sorts of contexts without objection. In fact, we embrace it. We want objective judges. We want objective juries. We want police officers to be objective in how they make arrests and detectives to be objective in how they evaluate evidence. We want doctors to be objective in their diagnoses. We want scientists to be objective in their research; for example, in developing new drugs and therapies.
>
> Somehow, the concept of "objectivity" is fine and appropriate—even mandatory—when we assess the performance of other professionals. Suddenly, the term is anathema among many journalists, especially a younger generation, when applied to ourselves. We must think very little of ourselves as a profession if we feel incapable of achieving the very standards we expect of others who

hear testimony, examine documents and conduct independent research.

Objectivity doesn't mean both-sidesism. It doesn't mean balance. It doesn't mean neutrality or false equivalence. It does mean open-mindedness. It does mean a willingness to listen and learn. It does mean being thorough in our research. It means not thinking we start with the answers but rather that we go seeking them. It represents an acknowledgment on our part that what we know, or think we know, pales in comparison to what we don't know (and even may not have thought to ask). We should recognize that we as journalists are often seeing the world through a keyhole. Objectivity represents an acknowledgment that much can be out of sight, that we need to work hard to see what might be missing from view and that what's out of sight could alter our understanding.

When we've done our work with requisite rigor and thoroughness (also known as solid, objective reporting) we should tell people what we've learned and what remains unknown—directly, straightforwardly, unflinchingly—just as people in lots of other professions do when they're doing their jobs correctly. That's what "objectivity" was intended to mean when the term was developed for journalism more than a century ago. That's what it really means today.

In keeping with that, I was impressed by some news organizations that decided to step outside the mainstream as they covered the aftermath of the 2020 election, particularly the relentless efforts by Trump and his allies to claim that he was robbed of a second term. *The Philadelphia Inquirer,* long one of the most respected regional newspapers in the country, made a choice that I found both sensible and courageous. The paper decided not to use the word "audit" when referring to a bad-faith effort by Pennsylvania Republicans to investigate the 2020 election in their state. Editors made that choice because, as they told their readers, there was no indication that the Republicans' effort "would follow the best practices or the common understanding of an audit among nonpartisan experts." What it *did* follow was months of demands from Donald Trump for an investigation that would give weight to his false claim that the election was rigged. But there was nothing to back that up. Biden won the state by more than eighty thousand votes. County and state audits had already affirmed that outcome, and no one had turned up any meaningful fraud. What the *Inquirer* was doing was, in fact, not slanting the news by refusing to use the Republicans' language, but remaining true to actual reality. "We think it is critical to speak plain truths about efforts to make it harder to vote and about efforts to sow doubts about the electoral process," the paper's senior politics editor, Dan Hirschhorn, told me. "There is clear, objective truth here."

Another Pennsylvania news organization, WITF—the all-news public radio station in Harrisburg—made a similar decision. They didn't want to let the lies about the election, or the attempts to overturn it, simply get shoved down the memory hole. They decided they would remind their listeners, and the readers of their website, about how their elected officials had behaved. So in late January 2021, just weeks after the Capitol insurrection, the station posted an explanatory article stating that they would be regularly reminding their audience that some state legislators had signed a letter urging Congress to vote against certifying the state's election results, and that some members of Congress had voted against certifying the state's election results for President Biden, even though there was no evidence to support the claims of election fraud. In essence, the station was merely reminding its audience that these politicians had knowingly spread misinformation—in other words, they had lied—in an effort to give Trump a second term. The language was forthright: "This was an unprecedented assault on the fabric of American democracy."

"We struggled, because this is not the normal thing," Scott Blanchard, one of the editors who helped make the decision, told me when I interviewed him for my column. "We had to ask ourselves, 'Does this mean we are not independent journalists?'" In other words, the objectivity question had reared its head. Wouldn't they be seen as biased? Was this really the neutral coverage that is so prized in mainstream journalism? After a lot of discussion, the editors and their reporters came to believe that accountability was more important than the supposedly neutral practices to which so many news organizations are wed.

But it was a little scary. "We're out on a ledge here," another WITF editor, Tim Lambert, recalled thinking. They hoped that other news organizations would follow their lead, but what happened was quite the contrary: "It's been radio silence." How long would WITF keep this up? At least through the 2022 midterm elections and possibly through 2024. "Elected officials are going to run on this," Blanchard said as he explained the reasoning. "This is an example of their judgment."

I wrote columns about all of these decisions—Andrew Taylor's to quit the AP, the *Inquirer*'s not to use the word "audit," and WITF's to keep up the reminders—because they were rare. Most journalists and most news organizations didn't stray beyond the traditional ways. In addition, there was so much pressure to appear objective that they didn't want to join the others out on that ledge. But in my view, that fealty to the status quo was part of the reason that by the fall of 2021 millions of Americans had bought the lie about the supposedly stolen election.

The Reuters Institute, a think tank and research center based in the United Kingdom and affiliated with Oxford University, decided to take a sweeping look at this question of objectivity. Their researchers interviewed news consumers in Great Britain, Germany, Brazil, and the United States about their news preferences, specifically on the issue of impartiality. Their findings, released in the fall of 2021, were clear. Impartiality was still a very high value, but most people believed they weren't getting it: "Defenders of impartiality point to a continuing need for unbiased news that fairly represents different viewpoints in a world where extreme opinions, bias and misinformation is more available than ever." This is no surprise, of course. But maybe the key word here is "fairly."

Is it representing news *fairly* to give climate change deniers and vaccine skeptics equal time with those who base their views and actions on science and reason? Do we really want to split things down the middle and call that public service? The report does call for one major change: News, analysis, and opinion should be labeled more clearly so that consumers can readily tell if what they are reading or watching is meant to be coming from a specific point of view or if it's intended to be completely impartial. That's especially important in digital contexts, where all of these forms of journalism come at us in a never-ending flow of content, usually arriving via social media. The way news and opinion come at the audience now is a far cry from the old days of print newspapers, when the front page was for straight news, staff-written opinion pieces appeared on the editorial page, and other points of view were on the opposite (or "op-ed") page. Smartphones and laptops make no such distinction, nor does Facebook's news feed or Twitter's timeline. It's just a firehose spouting "content." A summary of the study did give a nod or two to some of the related issues roiling newsrooms: "While showing greater empathy is increasingly expected by a younger generation and can be compatible with impartiality, this should not tip over into taking sides in news reporting."

When I was running the *Buffalo News* newsroom, I discouraged staff from displaying their political beliefs. Although I never wanted to strictly forbid staffers from, for example, taking part in a march for or against abortion rights—a hot subject during my tenure—I sometimes asked them not to do so. I don't remember any instance of anyone ultimately flouting my request, but certainly I do remember some emotionally charged conversations. Could I have ordered them not to march or have a political sign on their lawn? Possibly, but I was trying to walk a line in which I respected their civil liberties and still protected the paper's reputation for impartiality. If Twitter had been more dominant then, that would have made it much more challenging.

Neil Barsky, the former *Wall Street Journal* reporter who in 2014 founded The Marshall Project, a nonprofit news organization dedicated to criminal justice reform, had worthwhile ideas on this subject. When he stepped down as Marshall Project chairman in 2021, he wrote a moving memo to the staff. "The tension between advocacy and journalism never goes away, and from time to time, I have heard people say we are too partisan or not partisan enough. Here, I am unwavering: Despite my strong personal views about the rancid criminal justice system, I am certain that our work will have the greatest impact only if it is independent and nonpartisan," Barsky wrote. But he drew a distinction between being nonpartisan—that is, not affiliated with any political party—and the notion of objectivity, which seemed to him to demand having no point of view at all.

"I don't believe 'objectivity' is achievable or desirable, and I don't think reporters need to check their humanity at the door while doing their jobs," he wrote. "But I do believe in fairness. I believe in letting the facts we uncover determine our conclusion rather than the other way around." (This is Baron's view, too, though Barsky rejects the word "objectivity.") Barsky urged the staff never to lose their sense of outrage over a criminal justice system that is terribly unfair.

"Despite some favorable developments over the past several years," he wrote, "the American criminal justice system remains a national disgrace. In my opinion, our courts, jails, police forces and prisons (also housing, education, transportation systems and more) greatly favor rich over poor, White over Black or brown. In other countries, this situation might be called a caste system or apartheid. It is easy to become numb to brutality, dehumanization and racism." In the six years after its founding, Barsky's nonprofit newsroom took home two Pulitzer Prizes, quite an accomplishment for a journalistic start-up. Like ProPublica, it was clearly coming from a point of view. Its journalism flowed from the belief that the criminal justice system is deeply flawed and needs investigative journalism to shine a light in order to bring about reform.

Whenever I dared to suggest, in my columns or in media appearances, that a new way of thinking about objectivity might be necessary, I would be disingenuously attacked from the right. ("Margaret Sullivan wants even more leftist bias from leftist media" was the gist.) I knew that I was independent and nonpartisan. I hadn't belonged to a political party in several decades, which meant I couldn't vote in primary elections. When I heard friends or relatives talking about what "we" need to do—meaning people with progressive views—I would often correct them. I'm not on the team. I'm not part of that "we." Still, I was often branded by conservatives as a raging liberal or a tool of the Democratic

National Committee, working off DNC talking points. That bothered me, but I knew I couldn't let it change my writing or my convictions.

I learned to shrug it off. I knew that I was right when, in a 2021 column for the *Post,* I wrote that Big Journalism (broadcast TV networks, the dominant national newspapers, the major cable networks) needed to have an open-minded, nondefensive recognition of what had gone wrong in politics and news coverage. I wasn't terribly hopeful because, as I wrote, mainstream journalists want their work to be perceived as fair-minded and nonpartisan. They want to defend themselves against charges of bias. So they equalize the unequal in a practice that seems so ingrained as to be unresolvable. But I urged them to get over it. Democracy itself depended on it.

Reporters for magazines and other publications with a clear political perspective were already doing this. Ari Berman, the excellent voting-rights reporter for *Mother Jones,* even touted this philosophy in a fund-raising letter to subscribers and would-be subscribers: "Being funded by readers like you means that I can give a damn, too—and not just dispassionately chronicle the brazen attacks on the foundation of our democracy as normal run-of-the-mill news." He emphasized that the spate of legislation that would suppress voting or even help a second effort to overturn a legitimate election should never be depicted as "partisan bickering." Berman was talking about extreme gerrymandering to redraw election districts for political purposes, about voter suppression efforts, and about replacing honorable secretaries of state with partisan actors willing to abdicate their responsibilities for political purposes.

But the mainstream press? Big Journalism? Many of its practitioners seemed far more reluctant to look this pressing issue in the face. In the fall of 2021 I asked representatives of the three major broadcast networks why they had essentially ignored the so-called Eastman Memo, the shocking six-point legal blueprint that a Trump lawyer wrote in order to coach Vice President Mike Pence on how to overturn the 2020 presidential election. Some of them told me they didn't think it was much of a story. After all, as one put it, what Eastman was proposing in his memo never came to pass. So, apparently, there was nothing to worry about. Meanwhile, the networks devoted nearly endless airtime, that very week, to the compelling but far less important story of Gabby Petito, the twenty-two-year-old woman whose remains had been found in Wyoming after she had gone missing. There was something really wrong with the media's priorities. I thought the Eastman Memo should have been a flashing warning sign, proof that Donald Trump's allies were planning the end of fair elections in America. Maybe the major media organizations were ignoring it, in part, because they didn't want to be seen as partisan. Was this kind of news judgment the result of the media's endless homage to objectivity?

Perhaps it's better to reframe this discussion by emphasizing words like "fairness," "impartiality," and "independence." The Reuters study, which surveyed not just the United States but also Germany, the United Kingdom, and Brazil, found that respondents used the words "objectivity" and "impartiality" almost interchangeably, and they put a high value on both. One young participant in the United Kingdom put it this way: "The way I see impartiality is like being fair, that is how I would define impartiality. Even when a judge is listening to a case he is not swayed, he has just come there open-minded and then he is listening to both sides and then he makes a decision."

Certainly, the ideals of independent, impartial reporting are worth holding to, whether it's called objectivity or simply open-mindedness and fairness. I would, however, point out that what people *say* they want, in an interview or survey, is not always what they seek out.

In real life, they actually click on content that makes them feel a strong emotion—like outrage or anger—or that feeds a preexisting belief. This is much of the basis of hyperpartisan media on both the left and the right. Outrage sells. Tell me what I want to hear, whether it's strictly true or not. This is why Fox News's Tucker Carlson is so popular, and it's why some of the most popular Facebook pages are those from people like Ben Shapiro and Dan Bongino, right-wing commentators who stir strong emotions in order to keep their audience hooked. The overkill coverage of the infamous Steele Dossier's unverified claims about Trump is more evidence of the demand for outrage-inducing coverage, even when unconstrained by the facts. Many of Trump's enemies and critics desperately wanted to portray him as a Russian agent. They latched on to anything that suggested such a thing, hoping revelations along those lines would bring him down.

News consumers may *claim* they want neutral reporting and information: "Be objective. Just give me the facts."

But their behavior isn't always consistent with that. In their choices of what to watch, read, and listen to, Americans often live comfortably ensconced in echo chambers resounding with emotionally charged opinions just like their own. Navigating that is a major challenge—mostly an unmet one, so far—for the reality-based press in a democracy that's teetering on the brink.

Related to all of this is a question that has increasingly roiled newsrooms. Should journalists be allowed to cover things they have strong personal feelings about (for example, transgender rights) or personal experience with (such as having been a victim of racism or sexual assault)?

That issue came up at *The Washington Post* in a way that rocked the staff and created discussion far beyond our paper. In the summer of 2021, a *Post* reporter, Felicia Sonmez, sued her employer and five senior editors, as well as Baron, who had retired at the beginning of the year. Her suit claimed that these editors had discriminated against her by preventing her from covering stories about sexual assault because she was a victim of such assault herself. Sonmez, a national politics reporter, wanted $2 million in damages to her career, to her mental and emotional health, and to her rights to equal employment. Her detailed claims, including many specific quotations from the editors, were stunning. According to the suit, Cameron Barr, the *Post*'s managing editor, had told her she had "'taken a side on the issue'" by going public about her own experience. For days after the suit was filed, many of us at the *Post* could talk about little else, though most conversations were moved off Slack (the messaging system used within the *Post*) and onto encrypted messaging services like Signal.

I felt torn. I had a great deal of loyalty to Baron and some of the other editors, whose journalism I admired and who had treated me supportively, including when my work was under fire. As a former top editor myself, who had dealt with thorny staff complaints, I could imagine how awful it would be to be sued by an unhappy employee and to have my every intemperate remark or ill-considered email made public. And I knew that in personnel matters, there's often a lot that managers can't say.

If I had ever met Sonmez, it was only in passing. The *Post*'s newsroom is a big place, with more than one thousand staffers, and she and I worked on different floors and in different departments. We'd had a little bit of contact over the years by email or in direct messages on Twitter. Because I've always tried to be helpful to younger journalists, especially women, and because, like Felicia, I had been the object of frightening online threats and abuse, I felt supportive of her. I had written columns about how women journalists are targeted online and about the psychological toll that takes. I understood that at a personal level. So although I didn't know her well, I found myself sympathizing, at least in some ways.

It certainly seemed an extreme measure for the *Post* to have suspended her in early 2020 after she tweeted a link to an article shortly after NBA superstar Kobe Bryant died in a helicopter crash with his daughter and seven others. The tweeted article, without any commentary from Sonmez, detailed the sexual assault allegations against Bryant from years before. At that moment, Bryant was being not just mourned but almost canonized in the immediate post-crash coverage, and Sonmez was clearly making a point that there was another aspect to remember. She brought an extra awareness to this, she has said, because she experienced sexual assault herself. But Bryant's multitudes of fans were disgusted by her tweet, especially given the timing immediately after his shocking death.

When she was swamped online with rape and death threats because of that, a *Post* editor suggested Sonmez stay with a friend or get a hotel room but, according to the suit, didn't provide or offer security. Soon after, she was put on paid leave—suspended, in other words—apparently on the grounds that she had violated the *Post*'s social media policy. Many newsroom staffers were outraged. They got together to support her strongly and in writing. The journalists' union, the Guild, circulated a petition that garnered hundreds of signatures. The *Post* soon ended the suspension and Sonmez returned to work.

The lawsuit also detailed how, at various times over several years, she was barred from covering some stories related to sexual assault, including Christine Blasey Ford's sexual misconduct allegations against Supreme Court nominee Brett Kavanaugh. Overall, Sonmez described a hostile work environment that hurt her and hindered her career. Reading the suit—particularly the disparaging or insensitive comments she said that high-ranking editors had made to her—was a startling experience. Equally shocking was the idea that a reporter would be angry and miserable enough to sue the news organization where she still worked. It hit many other journalists, especially women, the same way.

Months later, the *Post* filed a motion to dismiss the case. It argued that the editorial decisions to keep her away from certain coverage areas were the result of Sonmez's "public advocacy." The editors' decisions weren't about gender discrimination or Sonmez's background but rather were made to prevent any perception of bias. The *Post*'s motion called the case "nothing more than the continuation of a campaign [by Sonmez] against the journalistic and editorial policies" of the *Post.* In March 2022, D.C. Superior Court judge Anthony Epstein dismissed the suit, saying that Sonmez had not demonstrated that the *Post* showed "discriminatory motive" in making her reporting assignments, and that the paper was merely trying to maintain a public image of unbiased news coverage. Sonmez, through her lawyer, responded that she strongly disagreed with the judge's reasoning and that she would appeal his ruling. The whole episode was a strong indication that the relationship between newsroom leadership and rank-and-file staff had changed radically and permanently.

For many reasons, top-down management was less accepted. Some of this was generational; younger journalists were used to sharing their opinions and to absorbing those of others, instantly available on social media. Then, too, there was a widespread and growing feeling that—given the political, racial, environmental, and economic upheaval in the nation and world—the stakes were so high that it was wrong *not* to speak out.

In many newsrooms, issues of racial diversity and equity were at the heart of staff discontent. At *The Philadelphia Inquirer*, top editor Stan Wischnowski resigned after an uproar over an article on vandalism that carried the headline "Buildings Matter, Too"—an insensitive play on "Black Lives Matter" that seemed, however inadvertently, to mock the movement for racial justice. The internal reaction to that headline was immediate. Some *Inquirer* staffers called off work "sick and tired," explaining in a written protest that they were "tired of shouldering the burden of dragging this 200-year-old institution kicking and screaming into a more equitable age. . . . we're tired of being told of the progress the company has made, and being served platitudes about 'diversity and inclusion' when we raise our concerns."

The top opinion editor at *The New York Times,* James Bennet, resigned after his section published an editorial by Senator Tom Cotton of Arkansas, "Send In the Troops," which suggested using the U.S. military to quell violent protests in American streets after the death of George Floyd in Minneapolis. Many Black journalists at the *Times* were among those who found the piece not only inflammatory but threatening to their safety. Previously, Bennet had been a leading candidate to succeed Dean Baquet as executive editor.

Both the Bennet and Wischnowski resignations struck me as extreme outcomes, although when Bennet admitted that he hadn't even read the Tom Cotton piece before it was published, I did doubt his management skills. He should have made clear to his lieutenants long before this incident that anything so sensitive needed to be brought to him for his explicit sign-off. As always with such departures, there was more to the story than merely the precipitating event. Bennet had made a major editing mistake in an editorial in 2017, bringing about a most unwelcome defamation suit by former Alaska governor and vice presidential candidate Sarah Palin; and the unhappiness on the *Inquirer*'s staff had been mounting for years.

The controversy I mentioned earlier over the prominent science writer Donald McNeil caused lingering rancor at the *Times,* too. The anger from many of his colleagues about his uttering the "*n*-word" during a discussion about language with high school students was worsened by the way top editors didn't take complaints about what had happened seriously at first. McNeil (by his own description a prickly personality) could have made things better by fully apologizing and owning his error, but he initially resisted doing so. The outcome seemed to me like overkill; surely, the discipline could have been handled with a less draconian result—although I certainly had no sympathy for any white person uttering the *n*-word, especially as a representative of the paper while on a trip with teenagers, as McNeil was.

On balance I thought the newsroom reforms and self-examination were necessary—even overdue. The *Los Angeles Times,* where particularly strong protests over diversity, equity, and inclusion came from staff, published a thorough exploration of the paper's deeply flawed history of covering communities of color. "Our reckoning with racism" included something rare in journalism—an apology to readers.

Perhaps surprisingly, given my age and long experience in newsroom management, I found myself in sympathy with those demanding radical change. Often, I was on the side of what was disparagingly and falsely called the "woke mob"—the younger, more diverse staffers who were supposedly running roughshod through Big Journalism's newsrooms. I had learned enough after my mistake covering the City Grill shootings in Buffalo to understand how poorly traditional journalism had served some segments of our community, and how insular and insensitive we could be. Traditional journalism, however revered in some circles, hadn't always served its readers very well.

For many years I had believed deeply in staff diversity and in fair pay and equal access to career promotion, and I had acted on that. I was proud to have appointed a Black woman, Lisa Wilson, as the top sports editor at *The Buffalo News*—a rarity in the nation—and to have hired Dawn Bracely as the first Black woman to join our editorial board. I had named Rod Watson the first Black editor in newsroom management.

At the *Times*, I respected the work of Nikole Hannah-Jones, liked her very much personally, and was disgusted to see the racist rancor coming at her after the publication of "The 1619 Project," the Sunday magazine's reframing of America's history to put more emphasis on the consequences of slavery and on the contributions to society of Black Americans. Her introductory essay won the 2020 Pulitzer Prize for commentary, and it kicked off an incredible furor among those who refused to make room for what it had to say. Despite the pushback (a tiny portion of which was grounded in objections by a few historians to some of the project's assertions), it accomplished its goals: Whether they accept it or not, many more people—in the United States and around the world—are aware of this neglected and ignored history than before Hannah-Jones began to write about it.

If "woke" meant being fully conscious of all of this, I

was for it. If "mob," a misnomer, meant that staff finally had enough strength in numbers to force long-delayed change at hidebound institutions, I could get behind that, too. What it all amounts to is this: Every norm of journalism is being challenged, and that is playing out in newsrooms every day. The industry itself is in turmoil, and the changes brought about by the pandemic—working remotely, for example—are adding to that. All these changes will shape the next decade and beyond of journalism, of its role in society, and its relationship to the public it serves.

13

How to Clean Up the Mess We're In

In early 2021 I taught a media ethics course at Duke University, provocatively titled "The News as a Moral Battleground." The class could just as easily have been called "Ripped from the Headlines." The twenty or so undergraduates, many of them public policy majors rather than journalism students, had plenty of compelling current events to consider. At this fraught moment in American history, not just the news was a moral battleground; the whole country had become one. Deeply woven into the stark division among citizens was the public health reality that the coronavirus pandemic hadn't abated. Hundreds of thousands already had died in the United States, but the vaccines hadn't yet arrived for the general public. The nation was at war about mask mandates, school policies, unemployment rates, and business lockdowns. The contentious presidential election had just concluded, followed by Donald Trump's appalling antidemocratic charges that he couldn't possibly have lost, so therefore the election must have been fraudulent and rigged.

The January 6 insurrection and riot at the Capitol, surely one of the hinge events in all of U.S. history, was fresh in our minds as we started the semester. Then, in the first few weeks of the class, Trump's second impeachment, on charges of inciting that mayhem, got under way. In the midst of all this, Biden's inauguration took place, with huge swaths of the nation convinced he wasn't the real president, and the right-wing news media playing along. In January, *New York* magazine graphically expressed the unending havoc by featuring three oversized words on the cover: "Insurrection. Impeachment. Inauguration." A phrase in tiny red letters nodded to the bizarre timing: "3 Wednesdays in America."

Even though I had run a newsroom after 9/11, and during a long period when a local battle was raging over abortion rights, I couldn't remember a time as tumultuous as this one. It was made more so by the knowledge that so many Americans not only believed the blatant lies about the election, but were beginning to believe the equally blatant lies about the riot itself—that it was caused by left-wing fanatics or that it really wasn't that major an event.

Trust in the legitimate press was at nearly its lowest point ever. In 2021, Gallup measured public trust in the media at 36 percent overall; it was much higher among Democrats and somewhat higher among independent voters, but only 11 percent of Republicans trusted the mainstream press.

This was the background of my Duke class. Because many students weren't on campus due to the pandemic, it needed to be taught entirely on Zoom. We met only once a week, on Monday afternoons, so each class was scheduled to be three hours long. A pure lecture format would have been sleep-inducing and dreary. I knew we desperately needed discussion, stimulation, and variety.

With that in mind, I almost always brought in a guest speaker, and was lucky enough to be able to lure prominent journalists of various generations whom I'd gotten to know over the years. Among the guests—and perhaps most memorable for me—was a less familiar name, unless you happened to be a close follower of Pulitzer Prize winners and investigative reporting. This was Alan Miller who, as a reporter at the *Los Angeles Times,* mostly in the 1990s, had done important investigative reporting, including revelations about illegal political contributions to the Democratic National Committee to support Bill Clinton's reelection. Later, with his reporting partner Kevin Sack, he investigated the dangers of a variety of Marine Corps jet that had been linked to the deaths of forty-five pilots. (Chillingly, that aircraft was so dangerous that it bore a nickname: "The Widow Maker.") Miller and Sack won the Investigative Reporters and Editors Medal and the 2003 Pulitzer Prize for National Reporting. By the time Alan Miller came to my class, he hadn't been a newspaper reporter for quite a while, despite his remarkable skills. His career took a radical turn in the mid-2000s after a visit to the school where his daughter was in the sixth grade. He spoke to the students about the crucial role of good journalism and the importance of learning to become well-informed citizens, and afterward received 175 thank-you notes. The enthusiastic response was part of what propelled him to leave the newsroom where he had worked for two decades and do something radically different. He founded the News Literacy Project, a nonprofit organization whose mission was to help students tell lies from truth, fiction from fact, all within a news environment that was rapidly deteriorating. Local newspapers were dying; hyperpartisan media was substituting outrage for truth; mainstream media was hungry for audience share to boost profits.

My media ethics students were always extraordinarily polite and respectful, but one student asked Miller a challenging question that might have seemed a little rude. Is what you're doing really *effective*? she wanted to know. Can your organization really make a difference, given all the misinformation and mistrust, amid all the lies, and all the politicized nonsense that tries to present itself as news? Miller clearly had thought a great deal about this, and he answered directly. What he and his team were doing, he had once acknowledged to interviewer Ted Koppel, "was like trying to empty the ocean with a teaspoon." Even so, Miller felt that there was no other choice but to try; the work is vital if American democracy is going to survive. The class and I found it hard to disagree.

I was moved by his appearance in my class. His sentiments corresponded closely with my own observations, but, as a columnist for *The Washington Post,* I was still seeing the ugly damage to democracy from the inside. Although my job was to observe and persuade, I knew that I was no longer able to change readers' viewpoints; with very few exceptions, their minds were made up.

I couldn't help but feel we were in real trouble, and I have serious doubts about whether America's news media will be up to the task and whether the level of most Americans' news literacy—the ability to tell lies from truth in the media—is high enough to support our system of government by the people. How do you battle against the social media algorithms that incentivize lying and outrage for the sake of profit? How do you introduce factuality and reason, not to mention civility, into disagreements that are getting more tribal all the time? In short, what can we do about it?

While I am worried and discouraged, I believe we can improve the situation by pressing ahead on four fronts, which to some extent are interrelated. First, the reality-based press has to reorient itself, framing its core purpose as serving democracy, not chasing clicks or fomenting outrage, not building egos or winning prizes, not worshipping corporate profits. Top editors need to take this goal seriously and communicate it to their staffs at every turn. I'll return to this.

Second, those who care about truth must do everything in their power to minimize the harm caused by those media outlets and platforms that traffic in lies and conspiracy theories. Accountability is paramount. Responsible lawsuits, like those of Dominion Voting Systems against right-wing news organizations who allowed or encouraged their staffs to broadcast lies about election fraud, will be a necessary part of this. Advertising boycotts can help. So will efforts to reduce the revenue of news organizations that spread misinformation—Fox News, in particular—by limiting the amount of money they make from lucrative cable transmission fees. (There's a movement called "UnFox My Cable Box," which urges consumers to demand that their cable providers change the way they, in essence, subsidize Fox News.) Part of these efforts involves meaningful regulation to counter the excesses of the social media platforms—particularly Facebook, which is such a behemoth. One way to do this, as many reformers have suggested, is to cautiously amend Section 230 of the Communications Decency Act of 1996, which protects social media platforms and other tech companies from legal liability when they post things that are harmful or dangerous. Reforming it could have potentially serious repercussions for free speech; it's a tricky balance.

A high-profile commission at the Aspen Institute took six months to study the problem of what they called "information disorder." In late 2021 they came out with a report that included fifteen recommendations. These included urging elected officials to take this problem seriously and dedicate resources to it, protecting local news sources, and increasing newsroom diversity in order to build public trust. It called for more transparency from large technology companies and for changing laws that shield digital platforms, like Facebook, from being held legally responsible for the content they magnify and amplify via their algorithms. As noted, all of this has to be carefully balanced with preserving free speech, but First Amendment concerns shouldn't be used as an all-powerful shield against regulation. The commission's study and its proposed solutions are worthwhile reading for anyone who is concerned about these problems, as we all should be; however, whether their recommendations have much chance of being widely adopted is another matter altogether. Reform, regulation, and leadership at the highest level are necessary, though hardly sufficient on their own, to deal with the scope of the disinformation and mistrust problem.

Third, in my view, we need a widespread effort to educate the public—not just schoolchildren but adults, too—about news literacy and about the deadly harm of not knowing the difference between truth and lies. The News Literacy Project, which has expanded to include adults, is a model; there are others springing up, and such efforts need to spread far and wide. It's important, too, for news consumers, also known as American citizens, to take responsibility for their own news literacy. I'm not terribly hopeful about this happening on its own, given the trends. I'm worried, too, about what it would mean to legislate it. Trying to get news literacy taught in public schools, given the turmoil over curriculum in recent years, could have unexpected negative consequences. I still think it's worth pursuing. I might even put Alan Miller in charge of it if I had the power.

And fourth—possibly the most important—we need to strengthen and shore up legitimate *local* news organizations, including, but not limited to, local newspapers. Study after study has shown that local news is relatively well trusted among a populace that increasingly disdains the national mainstream media. When local news fades, bad things happen in communities: polarization increases, civic engagement goes down, municipal costs go up. People retreat even further into political tribalism, not even able to talk to their neighbors about important concerns. How do we do this strengthening? This, too, has to happen on several fronts. Regular citizens should subscribe to or donate to news organizations in their communities; philanthropists and other powerful people should recognize how much is lost when these organizations fade away and do everything in their spheres of influence to help. That includes opening their own wallets and putting pressure on elected officials to pass legislation to provide relief.

I've been amazed and heartened by the good journalism I see done at the local level, even on staffs that have been so severely cut. I see that crucially important work at my former paper, *The Buffalo News*. I see it at papers like the *Times Union* in Albany, which did some of the most important investigations of sexual misconduct charges against former governor Andrew Cuomo. The challenges are unending, though. More than two thousand American newspapers went out of business between 2004 and 2020, and the trend hasn't stopped. Digital start-ups, including nonprofit newsrooms, increasingly—and admirably—are picking up some of the slack, but it's not nearly enough.

Again, this is personal. In late 2021, I was sickened when the dreaded news came that the chain that owned *The Buffalo News*, Lee Enterprises, had received an aggressive offer for its papers from the worst of the private-equity-based chains, Alden Global Capital. It was distressing enough that Warren Buffett, after decades of ownership, had recently sold the paper to Lee, itself a large chain, but I at least had some hope that, under Lee, the quality and staffing level would endure. There had even been some positive signs about the paper's profitability and digital-subscriber growth. I followed the *News*'s journalism closely, often admiringly, maintained ties to reporters and editors there, and, of course, was a subscriber. I took a seven-day print subscription in the summer months when I lived at a cottage on Lake Erie within the paper's circulation area. Everyone knew, though, that ownership by Alden would be tantamount to a death blow. That company is infamous for cutting newsroom staffs to the bone, chasing the highest possible profits, without regard for sustaining journalistic quality. It had happened in Denver, San Jose, and so many other places where robust newsrooms became ghosts of their former selves. Under Alden ownership, *The Buffalo*

News probably would survive in some form, but much of its quality journalism would not. For many of my friends and former colleagues this was personally frightening. It also was a symptom of a larger disaster, a deeply troubling trend visible everywhere in America, from which the dire effects on society were obvious.

The efforts to shore up existing local news outlets and to develop new ones deserve every bit of support that can be mustered. These include congressional action on tax credits to benefit local news organizations, philanthropy dedicated to digital start-ups, and ways to make it easier for legacy news organizations to turn themselves into nonprofit entities. There is, however, a strong sense of swimming against an inexorable tide, and almost a feeling of despair. Timothy Snyder, the celebrated Yale historian who wrote *On Tyranny*, has gone so far as to describe the decline of local news in the United States as the "essential problem of our republic."

Will these efforts get the job of saving democracy and curing misinformation done, if they all are somehow made to happen? Taken separately, no. If they are done simultaneously and with serious intentionality, though, America's democracy can survive. But it will take a mindset change, and for those in mainstream journalism it requires getting out of the inside-the-Beltway mentality.

Let's return to how the mainstream media can and must do better. First, they have to fully wake up to the challenge and to their role in it. If this is happening, it's happening slowly.

Too many journalists seem almost naive about the threats to democracy that they are enabling. Reviewing *Betrayal*, by ABC News chief Washington correspondent Jonathan Karl, about Trump's misdeeds before and after January 6, Jennifer Szalai of *The New York Times* mercilessly nailed what she found most notable about the book: the author's wide-eyed attitude about the president he had spent years covering. The book was packed with mini-scoops about Trump and his associates (for example, the way Trump loyalists purged anyone from the White House who would dare to disagree with the president), but that wasn't what struck the *Times* reviewer as the newsiest aspect. As Szalai put it, Karl's "expressions of surprise are so frequent and over-the-top that they are perhaps the most surprising parts of this book." She called the book "less insightful about the Trump White House and more revealing of Karl's own gradual, extremely belated awareness that something in the White House might in fact be awry." It made me wonder, too. Had Karl, one of the most prominent and experienced TV journalists in the nation, not noticed anything over the four preceding years? Perhaps chastened by this criticism, Karl later stated in a number of interviews that covering another Trump candidacy, replete with the former president's efforts to tear down democratic norms, would be a difficult challenge for political journalists, one they need to grapple with well before the campaign.

It's so rare for major news organizations to tell things through a clear, pro-democracy lens that when it happens, it's a cause for celebration. Consider this first sentence from a *New York Times* article: "Republicans in Wisconsin are engaged in an all-out assault on the state's election system." Eric Umansky, a high-ranking editor at ProPublica, commended it on Twitter: "Now *this* is how to write about our democracy." Why, though, is such straightforward clarity so unusual?

What I've found, in every newsroom where I've ever worked, is that reporters and editors are motivated by many things. There's competition—trying to get the scoop, to break the news first. This is a strong, impossible-to-extinguish drive that can't be separated from the kind of ambition that brings journalists to the highest levels of their business and, to some extent, it's a positive force. There's finding the biggest audience (or the most clicks); for some news organizations, that is less about clicks than about converting one-time readers to subscribers. But it often amounts to the same thing: getting the audience's eyeballs on your story and keeping them on your site. There's the desire to sound smart, savvy, and maybe a little jaded. There's the desire to win journalism prizes by writing stories—sometimes very long stories—that have gravitas and impact. There's the desire to look "balanced" and to avoid any accusations of bias, especially from often extremely aggressive right-wing critics.

I wrote about this frequently in my *Post* media column, calling for a new kind of framing. I identified what gets in the way. "Mainstream journalists want their work to be perceived as fair-minded and nonpartisan. They want to defend themselves against charges of bias," I wrote in one column. "So they equalize the unequal. This practice seems so ingrained as to be unresolvable."

Awareness of this has changed, but newsroom practices haven't followed suit to any great extent. How could this change be brought about? It would need leadership—patriotic leadership from the top of every major news organization, not the kind that involves mindless flag-waving but the kind that constantly communicates to staff and to the public what we're here for. I made some recommendations in my column:

- Toss out the insidious "inside-politics" framework and replace it with a "pro-democracy" framework. One way to do this is to establish new beats and teams of journalists to cover attacks on voting rights and other basic elements of a working democracy, and to treat this coverage as of utmost importance in how it is emphasized and displayed.
- Stop calling the reporters who cover what happens in Washington "political reporters." Start calling them "government reporters."
- Stop asking who the winners and losers are in the latest political skirmish. Start asking who is serving the democracy and who is undermining it.
- Stop being "savvy"—filled with smug insider knowledge—and start being patriotic. Again, I'm not talking about wearing American-flag lapel pins but about giving proper attention to the role of the press in a democracy, and letting the coverage reflect that.

I agree with Andrew Donohue, managing editor of the Center for Investigative Reporting's news site, Reveal, who in a piece for Harvard's Nieman Lab called for news organizations to put reporters on a new-style "democracy beat" to focus on voter suppression and redistricting: "These reporters won't see their work in terms of politics or parties, but instead through the lens of honesty, fairness, and transparency." But I called for something much more sweeping. The democracy beat shouldn't be some kind of narrow innovation but a widespread rethinking across the mainstream media.

Here's where I run into trouble about any likelihood of it happening. Big Journalism is notoriously bad at looking, in an open-minded way and without defensiveness, at what has gone wrong. If top editors were good at such things, we would have heard a lot more about the extreme overcoverage of Hillary Clinton's email practices and a lot more about how this can never happen again. We would have heard a lot more soul-searching, too, about how embarrassingly eager some of the Trump-as-Russian-agent speculators were—bearing in mind, however, that Russia certainly did intend to interfere in the 2016 election and did so. But improving this situation is not just about looking back; it's about anticipating what's to come next, and soon. What happens in 2024 if Trump runs again, with no intention of conceding loss even if the voters decide otherwise? Or if he doesn't, but a Trump-inspired candidate does the same?

Editors of leading news organizations, Sunday talk-show moderators, and other news executives should pull together their top people to think hard about this—every bit as hard as they think about digital innovation or increasing page views. They should be transparent and honest with their readers, viewers, and listeners about all of this. Some smaller news organizations have shown the way, quite admirably and bravely. I mentioned earlier that the Harrisburg, Pennsylvania, public radio station WITF clearly and consistently explained to their audience why they kept mentioning the actions of those public officials who tried to overturn the 2020 election results. Another model was *Cleveland Plain Dealer* editor Chris Quinn's letter to readers about how the paper and its sister website, Cleveland.com, refused to cover every reckless, attention-getting lie of Ohio Republican Josh Mandel during his run for U.S. Senate. Were these news organizations criticized for what they did? You can count on it. But that doesn't make it any less important or less correct.

There are good people thinking searchingly about these issues. Writing in The Bulwark in November 2021, Jonathan V. Last posed a question that should have sent chills down the spines of everyone who cares about this country, everyone with a patriotic bone in their body. "As we move toward 2024, the big concern should be how the media would cover an openly anti-democratic presidential candidate," he wrote. "Would they treat said candidate as a danger to America? Or would they attempt to remain neutral and pretend that he was just another generic politician doing normal political things?" If past is prologue, I'm afraid we already know the answer. That answer, though, is simply not adequate to the moment.

In late 2021 I got an unexpected email from the founder of a nonprofit organization dedicated to preserving democracy in the United States. He told me that his nonpartisan team was hoping to set up an event to explore how the media is, or isn't, adapting to the troubling dynamics within our democracy, and asked if he could send me a one-page draft of their proposal. I said I was happy to take a look at it, though I'm always wary of being on the "doing" side of things, accustomed as I am to staying strictly on the sidelines as an observer and commentator. When I received the proposal, I was surprised to see my name in the first sentence of the document. "This summer," it began, "Margaret Sullivan called for a widespread rethinking of how the media should cover issues related to our democracy, given the current political context facing the U.S." Well, he had my attention with that; the rest of the proposal would have captured it anyway. In partnership with a media platform or publisher, the organization wanted to host and support the production of an event, possibly at the National Press Club, with current and former journalists. The idea would be to foster conversation—among the practitioners of Washington journalism—about the media's current role, its responsibility, and the tools required to adequately cover today's political fights over elections, accountability for insurrection, and disinformation. This panel would look at "how media institutions can respond to changes in the industry and information landscape, and adequately cover today's democracy challenges in ways that are consistent with journalistic norms and practices." It would look at what's different about this moment in American history; what approaches various outlets are taking to covering issues, including January 6; disinformation, voting and election issues, and abuses of power. Ideally, there would be follow-up projects such as—and this is radical—an updated set of journalistic principles for threats to democracy in this era, or a sharing and highlighting of best practices.

I thought it sounded wonderful, but I told the founder that aspects of getting it done worried me. The very news organizations that most need to be involved would be resistant to participating. Why? Because it might make them look as if they were—horrors!—abandoning neutrality. The problem is a tautology, a Möbius strip looping around and around and ending up in the same place. To effect real change, you first must be willing to recognize the problem. Within the professional world I know so well, I doubt that there's a critical mass of powerful journalism leaders who want to do this. I was heartened—thrilled, in fact—when *The Washington Post* announced in early 2022 that it was starting a "democracy desk" that would put a good-sized group of reporters and editors on the story of American democracy in peril, with attention to voting suppression and the groundwork that's being laid to overturn elections in the future. Some of the reporters would be placed in the states that were most contested after the 2020 presidential election: Georgia, Arizona, Wisconsin, Michigan, and Pennsylvania. It's the kind of work that every serious news organization should be doing.

I gave my "Moral Battleground" class at Duke a daunting end-of-semester assignment. I asked them to imagine that they had been appointed Biden's anti-misinformation czar, the person responsible for solving these vexing problems of what has been called "truth decay." What would you do? Where would you start?

I didn't expect these students, bright and capable as they

were, to know all the answers, but I thought it would be worth having them think hard about the questions. They did, and overall, I was pleased with the way they grappled with the tricky intersection of public policy, social media reform, and free speech. Later that year, when the Aspen Institute released its report, I saw more developed and sophisticated versions of the same recommendations that my students had come up with, such as reforms that would hold social media platforms responsible for pushing lies, a big effort for media literacy, serious support for local news, and for government at the highest levels to treat these issues with the seriousness they deserve.

That the undergraduates in my class—many of them headed for public policy and journalism careers—were thinking so clearly and productively gave me tremendous hope. I also appreciated this surprising and provocative line in the Aspen Institute report about the seeming intractability of the problem: "The biggest lie of all, which this crisis thrives on, and which the beneficiaries of mis- and disinformation feed on, is that the crisis itself is uncontainable." That's right; it's not a lost cause, but citizens and leaders alike have to care enough to address it seriously and on many fronts simultaneously.

Amid all of this, I am somewhat encouraged by several developments. One is something mentioned briefly earlier: the growth of nonprofit digital-first newsrooms. One of the original and most successful ones, *The Texas Tribune*, is more than a decade old and does very important watchdog-journalism work for the entire state. Based in Austin, it is led now by Sewell Chan, whose background is in some of the largest newspapers in the country: *The New York Times* and the *Los*

Angeles Times. If every city and region in America could have its version of *The Texas Tribune,* I would sleep easier. But the problem is one of scale; how do you build a nationwide system to replace or augment newspapers? No one has solved that question yet, though many are working on it. The American Journalism Project, which directs philanthropy toward such newsrooms, has the right idea, as does the Institute for Nonprofit News and others that are focused on keeping local news alive in this new era.

I'm also encouraged to see some traditional local news organizations adjusting successfully to the new business realities. *The Salt Lake Tribune*'s ownership turned the newspaper into a nonprofit. The *Tampa Bay Times* and *The Philadelphia Inquirer* have somewhat similar structures, in that they are owned by nonprofit organizations. Some large, for-profit local newspapers—including *The Boston Globe,* the *Los Angeles Times,* and the *Star Tribune* in Minneapolis—have managed to maintain robust newsrooms and do outstanding work. It's notable that they share a particular, important characteristic: They have local, civic-minded ownership. Through that, they have escaped the grim fate of so many papers damaged by large chains.

The Washington Post, The New York Times, and *The Wall Street Journal* are a hugely important and influential part of this ecosystem. To varying degrees, each has figured out a new business model for the digital era, but they have something the smaller papers don't have—the ability to market their products to the entire nation and even, to some extent, to the world. I'm also heartened by the growth of investigative reporting at local television stations, and the positive role of public radio and television. These need to be encouraged and supported, too.

Underlying all of this is an article of faith for me. I believe that most legitimate journalists and millions of citizens know some truths at a core level: that we serve the public interest and that good journalism is foundational to democracy. That belief, I'm convinced, needs to come out from hiding. It should be boldly and consistently articulated and deeply supported. Above all, the reality-based press should rededicate itself to being pro-democracy. Then, I think, America gets a fighting chance.

14

About Those Lessons

In the fall of 2021, I found myself sitting on a Central Park bench with a young CBS News journalist, Jason Silverstein. We had been talking for nearly two hours, and I wondered if it might be time to call it a day. "Well," I asked him, "shall we wrap this up?" His answer startled me: "I'll take as much time listening to Margaret Sullivan as I can get." I really didn't think I was dropping any great pearls of wisdom, though we had been discussing a challenging new project of his and I had tried to provide some guidance. It wasn't terribly profound, mostly amounting to "Well, just get started, and you can always fix it later in the process." Jason and I went way back. He had been a correspondent for our *Buffalo News* teen publication, called *NeXt,* as a high school student in a Western New York suburb, and then was a standout summer intern at the paper during his college years. He had gone on to Columbia Journalism School and then to the New York *Daily News* and *Newsweek* before CBS News. (By 2022, some months after our talk, he had moved to *The New York Times.*) I was proud to know him, and touched that he made a point of keeping up with me; we'd had a number of these park walks in recent years.

That same week, I encountered another former *News* intern, Marcus Yam, a remarkably talented *Los Angeles Times* photojournalist who had just returned from Afghanistan. The access that this quiet young man gets to the ordinary people enmeshed in historic events, all over the world, is as remarkable as his photographs, each one like a beautifully composed Renaissance painting, glowing with humanity. Marcus has been part of two Pulitzer Prize–winning teams; by March 2022, he was in Ukraine, covering the Russian invasion. Just weeks later, he won a Pulitzer Prize for his photojournalism in Afghanistan. We were delighted to see each other at a Manhattan awards dinner, and I smiled to myself when—as a friend prepared to take a photo of us together—Marcus suggested a relocation. "Let's move over here," he said in his low-key way, and, of course, the lighting turned out to be perfect.

When people have asked me over the years whether journalism is still a good field for young people, I hesitate. Certainly, it's a tough one to break into, and an uncertain one in which to navigate a career. The *Buffalo News* teen publication where Jason started—*NeXt*—is no more, another victim of endless budget cuts, despite nurturing budding journalists like my Style section colleague Dan Zak, one of *The Washington Post*'s best writers. The internship program at *The Buffalo News,* where I began, as did Marcus Yam, Jason Silverstein, and Dan Zak, was discontinued several years ago (although, I was glad to see, it was brought back in 2022). No, I'm tempted to say, it's not a particularly good field. Then I think about Sophie, Alison, and Peter, three young journalists whose careers I've watched with particular interest over the years because I had a personal connection to each.

Sophie Kleeman, who was my daughter's college roommate, is an investigations editor at Business Insider; her career has been almost entirely with digital publications. Alison Ingersoll, my son's former girlfriend, is a data journalism specialist at WRAL, the NBC-affiliated TV station in Raleigh, North Carolina; she has worked not only in television but also for a local investigative nonprofit and, during an internship, at Bloomberg News in London. Peter Sullivan, my nephew, had internships with *Foreign Policy* magazine and at the *Pittsburgh Post-Gazette* and now covers health care in Congress for *The Hill.* Their paths have been various and mostly not based in print. All are roughly thirty years old, doing important work, and paying the rent.

"The most satisfying thing you'll ever do in this business is bring along young journalists," was what Douglas Turner told me. He had been the top editor of the *Courier-Express,* the Buffalo newspaper that went out of business in 1982, and later was the Washington bureau chief of *The Buffalo News.* Few of these young journalists are as straightforward as Jason Silverstein in seeking guidance, but I do get asked for advice from time to time. There are five things I've figured out over the years, often through my own errors.

First, I tell them to be patient with themselves, especially with career setbacks and mistakes. Like fiction writers who could paper the walls with their rejection letters, journalists find out quickly that this is a tough, competitive, often unforgiving field. There will be jobs you want that you won't get; that's happened to all but the very fortunate few. (I'm not even sure it makes them fortunate; that humbling can be good for the soul.) There very likely will be humiliating errors that you will be lucky to survive.

Longtime journalists, if they're honest, can tell you all about their disasters, failures, and disappointments. I wrote a front-page story at the *Buffalo News* in my first year on the job that was essentially wrong because it was based on calculations about real estate square footage; I did the math correctly but with the wrong assumptions about what it meant. I've never forgotten that screw-up or the embarrassment of correcting it after a miserable conversation in my editor's office. Persistence goes along with being patient with yourself. Try to hang in there, since memories are short and, if you're lucky, you'll probably get another chance to right yourself and your reputation.

Second, I would tell them this: Do your own work, and when you borrow or find inspiration elsewhere, be generous in crediting others. In our digital age, it's never been easier to plagiarize, even without intending to, and it's never been easier to discover plagiarism. All it takes in one case is sloppy copy-and-pasting; all it takes in the other is a Google search. I would add that there's a solution: It's never been easier to give credit. Link out, give a phrase of attribution, and then do it again and again. It's amazing that journalists don't do more of this; it's always appreciated and, in almost all circumstances, it takes nothing away from your own work.

Third, I'd suggest some self-discipline in the use of social media. It's so easy to get involved in the digital equivalent of road rage. Put the phone down, walk away from the keyboard.

An errant tweet can wreck your career. Delete all you want, but if someone captured a screenshot, your momentary bad judgment will live forever. Despite what you may think, exactly no one is eagerly awaiting your words of wisdom on any platform. I'd like to see journalists doing less to build their reputations ("brands," in the somewhat dated parlance) on social media or in television appearances and more of the actual work of rigorous reporting. I say this knowing that, for many journalists, especially ones not attached to prestigious legacy news organizations, such reputation building is a career necessity. And done right, it can be a positive thing.

But for some, at least, a more muted approach—grounded in dogged reporting above all—is preferable. An example of this in action is my *Washington Post* colleague Stephanie McCrummen, whom I have worked alongside in the *Post*'s New York City office. She keeps a low profile and rarely does anything self-promotional, but her byline on a story is a clear signal that the reporting will be deep, original, and worthwhile. It was no surprise to me that she won both a Pulitzer Prize and a George Polk Award in 2018 after her investigative reporting, with colleagues Beth Reinhard and Alice Crites. Their work changed the course of a Senate race in Alabama by revealing that the Republican candidate, Roy Moore, had behaved inappropriately with teenage girls and then had tried to undermine the reporting that exposed that behavior. McCrummen kept her cool when the undercover group Project Veritas, which bills itself as a media watchdog, tried to trip her up by offering a fake story; the video of that encounter is a model for good journalistic behavior in tough circumstances. McCrummen's list of well-deserved awards is exceedingly long, but her name isn't widely known. In short, show some restraint and concentrate on the work first.

Fourth, and maybe most important, hold on tight to the qualities that make a good journalist. Stay idealistic. Stay curious. Stay mission driven, and know how much it matters or can matter. Remember what happened when Darnella Frazier, only seventeen years old, decided to video-record the murder of George Floyd in Minneapolis as a police officer knelt on his neck; although she's not a journalist per se, she certainly performed a journalistic service. It was heartening to see the Pulitzer Prize board recognize her world-changing action with a special award.

My *Washington Post* colleague Meryl Kornfield wrote about the strange turn of events—again, involving a crucial video—that led to the convictions of the killers of Ahmaud Arbery, the twenty-five-year-old Black man in Georgia who was out jogging when he was gunned down by three white men. Much of the case came down to the persistence and curiosity of a reporter, Larry Hobbs, with *The Brunswick News*, a daily newspaper with only four reporters.

Reading Kornfield's story, I loved one quote from Hobbs. After obtaining the (extraordinarily biased and incomplete) police report, Hobbs knew he had to pursue the story. "Red flags start going up," he said. "All the things started falling into place that this wasn't right." Later, a cellphone video, uploaded to a local radio station's website, bore out his suspicions, as it showed men chasing Arbery, cornering him, and shooting him.

Hobbs's dogged reporting was not the only factor that led to the convictions, but it surely helped. Prosecutors and police were failing to do their jobs, but a reporter did his. With considerable modesty, Hobbs put it in perspective in the *Post* story: "The main thing I did was just not let go of it. I didn't do any great writing. I didn't do any investigative reporting. I'm a small-town newspaper. We don't really have time to invest. I come in every day and there's an empty newspaper I have to do my part to fill up."

In other words, he just did the work, guided by his instincts and persistence. Honor that reporter's instinct, which will hardly ever steer you wrong and which might serve the public interest in unimaginable ways.

I'll add one more: Try to work with people you admire, who respect you, and whom you can trust, especially those in leadership positions. If you value your co-workers, nurture the relationships as best you can. That includes managing the boss, a skill worth developing. When I was the top editor in Buffalo, I had my disagreements with my direct supervisor, publisher Stan Lipsey; I sometimes found him too involved in the newsroom—in wanting to direct stories—when I thought he should leave that strictly to me and my team. We worked out the differences, though, and generally communicated well. There were probably times when he wanted to fire me—in fact, he was fond of pointedly reminding me who really had the upper hand in the publisher-editor dynamic. When we disagreed, I held my ground and was much more secure in doing so because the relationship was strong. It didn't hurt a bit that we had a regular doubles tennis game on Wednesday evenings after work. (It's one thing to fire the editor, but much worse when you lose her killer first serve, too.) The important thing, and one reason we lasted together for nearly thirteen years in our respective roles, is that there was mutual respect. If that's not the case, and there's nothing you can do about it, I would advise getting out. That's hard—sometimes almost impossible—in an industry where jobs can be hard to come by. I'm sympathetic to those who, for financial or other reasons, can't make a move. But I also know that staying can be corrosive to your work and even to your soul.

15

Sweeney (and Other Legends), Reconsidered

A flashback: My earliest mentor at *The Buffalo News,* Foster Spencer, was one of those newsroom characters whose mere presence made it fun to come to work. The paper's longtime managing editor, Foster often said that he was content in his number two editorial position and had no desire to join the "executive team" by ascending to the top job of chief editor. He would rather put out the paper every day than go to meetings with bean counters. Although he wasn't strictly handsome, Foster's humor and intelligence nonetheless gave him charisma. I can picture him ambling out of the newsroom at day's end in his loden-green trench coat and tweed flat cap with the paper's final edition tucked under his arm. In that pre-Twitter, pre-smartphone era, his workday was well and truly over, and here was the proof, in print.

Foster had all kinds of entertaining expressions and ideas, like the name he gave to boring-but-important stories, such as a nearly interminable series titled "Zoning and You" that the paper had once published. He called them "FWS," which stood for "Fraught with Significance." In Foster's parlance, an exclamation point was "an astonisher," and a headline that stretched across all eight columns of the paper's front page was a "screamer." (Thus, when I broke a big story as a rookie reporter, Foster gave me due credit; after giving his directions to the editor laying out the front page, he called across the newsroom in his Massachusetts accent, "Sully, you got your first *scream-ah*.")

And then there was Sweeney, an imaginary character whom Foster was fond of invoking. Sweeney was the average reader, presumably a working-class guy sitting on his front porch in Irish Catholic South Buffalo, cracking open a Labatt Blue and picking up *The Buffalo Evening News* to see what it had to say. Foster kept him in mind when he made news decisions: *What would Sweeney think?*

Foster hired me as a summer intern, and then, apparently pleased with my work and hustle, offered me a full-time reporting job in September, breaking with the tradition that most *Buffalo Evening News* hires would have three to five years' experience at a smaller outlet. I was fired up and wanted to prove my worth. Not long after I was hired full-time, all of twenty-three years old, I approached him as he stood chatting with more senior reporters and told him with some excitement that I had just scored an interview with Joyce Carol Oates, the Western New York native and author who had already won the National Book Award for her novel *them*, which I had read in Joanne Langan's English class at Nardin Academy. Foster seemed to have only the vaguest idea of who she was, but he was supportive. "That'll be a good one, Marge," he said, using a nickname I would tolerate only from him. He had a characteristic way of speaking from the side of his mouth that made every utterance seem wised-up and wry.

I interviewed Oates after a talk she gave at a college campus, and then drove out to talk to her parents in nearby Niagara County, where she had grown up. The profile appeared as the cover story of our Sunday magazine. I remember my mother, who looked for my work as soon as the paper arrived at their Lackawanna door, telling me that *this* one was good enough to stand the test of time. She may have been right; I got a chance to recall it more than thirty-five years later when Oates and I met again in 2019. As I walked through the door of the writer Molly Jong-Fast's Upper East Side apartment for a book party, my first vision was of Joyce Carol Oates and Erica Jong, Molly's mother and the author of the culture-changing novel *Fear of Flying*. Seeing two of the most famous authors of their generation, getting on in years and chatting over cocktails, I felt I had arrived in literary heaven. On that Manhattan evening, Oates told me that she remembered my *Buffalo News* profile, and I reminded her that she had written me a kind note, saying how pleased she was to see her parents quoted in it.

Foster was only sixty-four, and still held the managing editor's title, when he died in Roswell Park Comprehensive Cancer Center. Still in my thirties then, I didn't realize how young he was, but I certainly do now, since it is my age as I write. I directly succeeded Foster as managing editor in 1998 and inherited his office, which I used for another fourteen years until leaving for *The New York Times*. I stayed there rather than moving into the chief editor's slightly superior quarters when I got the top newsroom job two years later. I liked being at Foster's old desk, scorched in places by cigarettes that were set down, I assumed, while he worked the crossword puzzle between deadlines.

A longtime colleague of Foster's, Edward Cuddihy, who eventually would hold the managing editor title himself, recalled the mythical Sweeney when he provided a comment for Foster's obituary. As Cuddihy assembled a journalism contest entry, Foster told him he didn't think much about awards: "If I can inform Sweeney and a half million of his neighbors, I've won the only prize I want."

Much as I adored Foster and was grateful to him, we didn't always see eye to eye in his last years. He looked askance at my proposed innovations, including the redesigned front page that helped propel my career even though it was never implemented, and wasn't shy about saying so. He probably would have been lukewarm about some of my other eventual efforts: my drive to diversify a newsroom staff that was far too white for our readership, not because he didn't fully support the goal but because it required modifying the paper's traditional hiring practices; my desire to give women's and girls' sports more attention despite their much smaller fan base; my directive to represent people of color and women on our front page as often as possible, even if that meant expanding time-honored definitions of newsworthiness. Those things may not have mattered much to Sweeney, but I thought they would matter to a readership that wasn't always well served by the old ways. I knew they mattered to me.

Not just Sweeney needs reconsideration in our greatly

changed era, I've found. Even the wonders of "Woodstein," the famed Watergate reporting duo of Woodward and Bernstein, demand a fresh look. Never meet your heroes, goes the saying attributed to Marcel Proust. I wouldn't take it quite that far. I'd just be prepared for some nuance to replace the idol worship. As I wrote in the first chapter here, I was a teen when the young reporters doggedly revealed the scandal; they cultivated that secret source, Deep Throat, and, partly through him, slowly uncovered the corruption of the Nixon administration. They were *badass*, the essence of swashbuckling cool, especially when confused in my teenage mind with Robert Redford and Dustin Hoffman, shirt sleeves rolled up and wide ties askew as they made coded phone calls to their sources or tangled with their demanding editor. I wanted to be them, or at least immerse myself in that newsroom culture. Righteousness could be achieved, according to the self-important journalism adage, by "afflicting the comfortable and comforting the afflicted." That sounded good. So I did what Thoreau advised, advancing not just confidently in the direction of my dreams but at something of a breakneck pace. In the summer of 1974, Richard Nixon resigned the presidency in disgrace, and in the fall I became the editor of my high school's student newspaper.

Later, as celebrity-journalists, Woodward and Bernstein were the star speakers or award recipients at conferences I attended, and on one occasion, probably in the 1990s, I introduced myself. They were well accustomed to such admiration. In more recent years, I ran into Carl Bernstein in a CNN greenroom as we were both waiting to appear on the media show *Reliable Sources*. By then, I was a columnist at his old paper, the *Post.* I made sure to get his phone number and interviewed him soon after, asking him to compare Nixon to Donald Trump. Bernstein talked brilliantly, if incessantly. (In his memoir, *All About the Story,* former *Washington Post* executive editor Leonard Downie observes of Bernstein that it was "almost impossible to break off a conversation with him, even over the phone.") I remember, too, running into Bernstein during the intermission of a Carnegie Hall concert. As my date stood by, suitably impressed, Bernstein greeted me with a kiss and told me I was "killing it" in my *Post* columns. My seventeen-year-old self, editor of the Nardin *Kaleidoscope,* would have found this scene gratifying if she could have begun to imagine it.

Woodward, though, drew more ambivalence. Certainly, he had had a remarkable career; his reporting work was still occasionally appearing on *The Washington Post*'s front page, five decades after his and Bernstein's initial Watergate reporting. He was a top-selling author many times over, with thick tomes investigating presidential administrations, the Hollywood drug culture, and the Supreme Court. But like too many other journalist-authors, Woodward sometimes saved some of the revelations from his research for those books instead of writing them as news stories in real time. (Downie acknowledged this tension in his memoir, writing that while some readers complained about Woodward's practice, "I never felt that our readers were cheated.")

In another strange turn, as surreal as my encounter with Bernstein though in a very different way, I would take up a Woodward controversy in the same newspaper where the former Watergate reporter still held the honorary title of associate editor. My column revolved around Woodward's second book about Donald Trump, published in September 2020. His first one, *Fear,* had been a major bestseller. This one, *Rage,* promised to be one, too—especially because it contained some startling news: That Trump *knew* early in 2020 that the coronavirus pandemic would be deadly, far worse than the flu. But as president, he blatantly lied about the severity of the virus's threat, assuring Americans that it was nothing to worry about, that it would disappear.

I decided to write about why Woodward hadn't reported this news months before his book came out. Why hadn't he talked it over with *Post* editors and arranged to break off some of his book's revelations for an immediate news story? I had Woodward's phone number and was able to reach him quickly. He sounded defensive and wanted to avoid speaking to me on the record. Instead, he suggested we talk "on background"—meaning that I couldn't attribute whatever he said to him directly. I wasn't interested in that since I was seeking his rationale for holding back the news. I insisted that I wanted his response on the record. We tussled about the terms of our conversation for a while, as he explained that he had promised CBS's *60 Minutes* the first interview after his book's publication. I held my ground, making it clear that if he didn't want to speak on the record, I would just note in the column that he had declined comment. That would not be a good look for a legendary reporter, especially one dealing with his own newspaper.

At one point, Woodward nonetheless started talking with these words: "On background . . ." I stopped him. "Please don't try to manipulate me into doing a background interview" was the sentence I heard myself saying to one of the world's most famous journalists and my teenage inspiration. He made it clear that he didn't appreciate my reaction and thought it was out of line, but in the end he did speak to me on the record.

My column carried this rather soft headline: "Should Bob Woodward Have Reported Trump's Virus Revelations Sooner? Here's How He Defends His Decision." My takeaway, though, was more pointed. I duly considered his arguments that his reporting was more meaningful in book form, that earlier publication would not have helped to save any of the two hundred thousand lives that had then been lost, and that voters could still consider Trump's duplicity well before election day, which Woodward called the "demarcation." But I concluded:

> I don't know if putting the book's newsiest revelations out there in something closer to real time would have made a difference. They might very well have been denied and soon forgotten in the constant rush of new scandals and lies. Still, the chance—even if it's a slim chance—that those revelations could have saved lives is a powerful argument against waiting this long.

One reader, a former U.S. ambassador during the Clinton years, wrote to me, angry about Woodward's rationale and objecting to the notion that the "demarcation" was the election. "No, it was as soon as Trump made his revelations to Woodward," the reader fumed. "Which almost surely, if they had appeared in print at the time, would have caused an uproar that would have led to demands across the country for changes in Trump administration behavior that would almost surely have saved thousands of American lives." Plenty of other readers accepted Woodward's reasoning and found my column pointlessly critical. But I felt good about getting him to state his case and about my conclusion.

As for my hero worship? I still admire the Watergate reporting, still am happy to have spent a life inspired by it and to have come to work at the same newspaper where this enduring and consequential journalism history was made. But I thought Woodward made the wrong decision and, what's more, I was disturbed to see the way he responded to journalists who questioned him at the annual Investigative Reporters and Editors (IRE) conference shortly after *Rage* was published. One of these was Shira Stein, a reporter for Bloomberg Law covering the pandemic; another was Karen Ho of Quartz. Both pressed Woodward, with more specificity than I did, about why he hadn't reported the Trump revelations earlier. He sounded dismissive, suggested they owed him an apology, and kept promoting his book. His behavior toward Jonathan Swan of Axios, who asked similar questions a few days later, was much more respectful. Maybe if Woodward had revealed the truth earlier and the nation had taken the virus more seriously early on, the IRE members would be meeting in person, not virtually. Maybe President Trump himself—who had for many months flouted social distancing recommendations and mocked mask-wearers—wouldn't have been hospitalized with Covid only a few days after Woodward's remarks to Stein and Ho.

That's the odd thing about reporting. You never know what will happen when you put the truth out there in real time. You might help banish a corrupt president, as Woodward and Bernstein did. Or you might shame another president into telling the truth about the worst public health crisis in American history. If that were to happen, you might help save thousands of lives. You don't know. And it's not your job to make that calculation. It's your job to dig it out and to tell it straight. And to publish without undue delay (as *The New York Times* infamously failed to do with the warrantless-wiretapping story in 2004).

The next year, Woodward came out with yet another Trump-related book, *Peril,* co-authored with *Post* reporter Robert Costa. Again, an excerpt appeared on the front page of *The Washington Post,* and again, I wrote a column about it. Woodward and Costa had unearthed the abhorrent memo written by a Trump lawyer, John Eastman, that gave Vice President Pence a detailed, six-point plan to declare the 2020 election invalid and falsely hand the presidency over to Trump. It amounted to a blueprint for the insurrection. I gave Woodward and Costa credit, and this time my point wasn't to quarrel with the timing but to complain that the Eastman Memo hadn't been treated as big news by most of the mainstream media. Shockingly, there was zero on-air news coverage on the three major broadcast networks of this revelation immediately after it was made public, according to a Media Matters for America study, and precious little in the following days. As our democratic norms foundered, much of the mainstream press was asleep at the switch, and seemed perfectly content to stay that way.

I heard from Woodward about my Eastman Memo piece. He had apparently let our earlier disagreement go, if he remembered it at all. "That was a terrific column," he wrote. "Thoughtful and aggressive." He gave me credit for prompting some follow-up coverage in *The New York Times.* (That credit was almost certainly undeserved; with a few rare exceptions, it wasn't like the *Times* to act on my advice.) I was glad that we remained on good terms. Proust notwithstanding, maybe it's not so bad, after all, to get to know your idols.

I have found, though, that the journalists I admire most aren't necessarily those with the biggest names or the best-selling books. The ones I have the greatest respect for are those—no matter how prominent or obscure—who are the most unflinching in seeking out the truth and presenting it straightforwardly. In the words of the classic *New York Times* axiom, they do their work "without fear or favor." Some of these are at major publications like the *Times* and the *Post;* others are in much smaller newsrooms or are fully independent. Some win Pulitzer Prizes; some don't get much recognition. As I mentioned in an earlier chapter, I admire Nikole Hannah-Jones of *The New York Times* for her bravery and vision in writing about the influence on American history of enslaved people's arrival in the English colonies in 1619, and her colleagues Jodi Kantor and Megan Twohey, who dug into film mogul Harvey Weinstein's sexual misconduct, revelations that led, in time, to his imprisonment. I admire the top editor of Albany's *Times Union*, Casey Seiler, who (while leading his paper's aggressive coverage of New York governor Andrew Cuomo's demise) insisted on keeping proper journalistic distance from sources, even if it hindered access. I give CNN's Jake Tapper credit for refusing to thoughtlessly magnify the voices of liars, as so many TV anchors do. I appreciate Will Bunch at *The Philadelphia Inquirer* for his incisive, pro-democracy commentary and Julie K. Brown at the *Miami Herald* for her persistent reporting about the disgraced financier Jeffrey Epstein, credibly accused of sex trafficking. There are far too many to list here, including many colleagues of mine, past and present, whose work inspires and awes me.

These days, however, I wonder if it's enough. A global study by a respected Stockholm-based think tank now describes the United States, for the first time, as a backsliding democracy. "The declines in civil liberties and checks on government indicate that there are serious problems with the fundamentals of democracy," concluded the International Institute for Democracy and Electoral Assistance. The "visible deterioration" of democracy in the United States includes the increasing tendency to contest credible election results, efforts to suppress participation in elections, and the country's "runaway polarization." This is not only true but obvious; it is staring us in the face.

American journalists should be putting the country on high alert, with sirens blaring and red lights flashing. The legitimate press should be trying to figure out how best to rise to this historic challenge. But too many journalists—worried about their reputations for neutrality, under pressure from corporate bosses, and mired in their comfortable traditions—are still doing their jobs the same old way. It's not good enough.

What if we did fully rise to meet the moment? Can an abundance of high-quality, mission-driven journalism overcome misinformation and break through to those indoctrinated in an alternative reality? Can the legitimate media—the reality-based press—ever recover lost public trust and credibility? I have serious doubts, but they don't make me completely disillusioned. I know that great journalism is powerful, that it can change the world. I'm worried, yes, but I remain moderately hopeful. For all kinds of reasons, I still believe in my craft.

And I still love practicing it, especially when I hear from readers like a woman in Texas who wrote to me after reading my *Post* column urging journalists and news organizations to refocus their coverage on the current threats to democracy. In Texas, she lamented, "democracy, voting rights and women's rights are pretty much DOA at this time." She offered some words of appreciation: "I want to take this opportunity to say thank you for your article on the importance of journalists speaking honestly and forthrightly on the attack on democracy in our country. While I'm not sure how much will change, I just feel a helluva lot better to see this articulated so honestly and directly in a major newspaper." Her brief note reminded me of why I've stayed in journalism for more than four decades. Some people get into journalism to expose corruption; others because they love to write; but for me, it's this relationship with the reader that means the most.

I'll conclude with a small story, a reconsideration of yet another legend. By the summer of 2021, I was getting burned out writing the media column. I had been doing it—at an average pace of two columns a week—for more than five years. I joked with my colleagues that there were really only five possible media columns, and I would write aspects of them over and over. There was the "Evils of Facebook" column; the one about the tragedy of local newspapers' decline at the hands of hedge-fund owners; the Fox News damage-to-society column; the "don't magnify political lies" column; and the one about the mainstream media's intransigent flaws. On the surface, my career was going well. I wrote a well-received book in 2020 and won a national award for my *Post* columns in 2021. Duke University's public policy school listed me as a faculty member. All of this was gratifying, but it didn't penetrate a deeper ennui.

Looking for variety, I started writing different kinds of pieces. One took up the reinvention of *Rolling Stone* magazine; another featured a new podcast that told the stories of inspiring people who were at least seventy years old. These were really feature stories, though, not opinion columns with a strong point to make. Readable, perhaps, but less important.

There was no denying that the Trump years had taken their toll on me, especially because of the distressing direction of the country, including the media's role in that, and because of all the nastiness and abuse that for years had been flooding my inbox, voicemail, and real-life encounters. The pandemic lockdown had isolated me from my newsroom colleagues. Even before that, I had isolated myself, to some extent, by moving back from Washington to New York City. I didn't regret that decision since New York suited me and endlessly fed my soul, but it did mean that I was only occasionally in the *Post*'s D.C. newsroom, working instead from the small New York City office. Once the pandemic hit, I worked solely from my Upper West Side apartment. Despite the burnout, I kept driving myself to write frequently, to keep going. It's what I had always done; but it was getting wearisome. I didn't want to admit it, but I was hitting the wall.

When I heard, via the newsroom's internal messaging system, from one of my favorite people, deputy features editor David Malitz, my curiosity was aroused. He surprised me by writing that he wanted to speak by phone—a rarity for him—about a story assignment. When we talked, Malitz said he wanted to send me to interview Joni Mitchell, the legendary musician who would soon be receiving a Kennedy Center lifetime achievement honor. I would fly out to California or British Columbia, depending on which of her homes she was living in, and spend a solid chunk of time with her. Then I would write a lengthy profile for the Sunday arts section. That sounded like a delightful change of pace, and a perfect fit. I had loved Joni Mitchell's music, as well as that of other singer-songwriters, for many years. Although I hadn't been on a plane in eighteen months because of the pandemic, I was vaccinated and more than ready.

There was just one problem. Joni Mitchell disliked interviews and mistrusted journalists. She felt burned by reporters who had sensationalized her comments or criticized her work without understanding it. At nearly seventy-eight, she wasn't in the best of health; she had suffered a brain aneurysm a few years earlier followed by a difficult recovery. So, after multiple conversations with her manager and her assistant, I was reluctantly ready to settle for something less than a lengthy in-person interview. A phone call. Or maybe a Zoom interview. Her staff took these ideas to her and the answer came back: a flat no. Nothing personal, but Joni Mitchell would not be talking to me. They offered me the option of emailing some questions to her assistant. If Mitchell chose to answer any of them, she would speak the answers aloud to the assistant, who would record, transcribe, and email them to me. Doing a written interview by proxy seemed an unproductive idea for this kind of personality-based story. Now it was time to think creatively, since the *Post* needed some sort of Joni Mitchell story to recognize her Kennedy Center honor. My colleagues were spending time with the other honorees, including Lorne Michaels of *Saturday Night Live* fame, legendary entertainer Bette Midler, and Motown founder Berry Gordy. I was the only one who had struck out, and the deadline was looming.

So I came up with an idea for a personal essay that wouldn't require Mitchell's cooperation. Her classic album *Blue* had turned fifty in 2021 and received endless recognition as one of the greatest of all time. My essay, though, would make the case that, excellent as it was, *Blue* wasn't her best. That had come three years later, I would argue, with *Court and Spark* in 1974. I listened anew to these albums and others, sometimes with musician friends helping me to hear them more perceptively. I remembered how much the album affected me as a young teen experiencing my first romantic turmoil, and I learned that Madonna had called *Court and Spark* her coming-of-age album. I got the chance to recall the harder-edged rock music that one of my older brothers, Phil, had introduced me to, like the Allman Brothers, the Rolling Stones, and The Who. Then I brainstormed with a colleague, movie critic Ann Hornaday, who offered an observation which I ended up quoting. *Blue* was like a glass of pure, cool water, Hornaday said, but *Court and Spark*, with its jazz-infused layers and glossy California production, was like a perfectly mixed tequila sunrise. A *Post* reader made me happy when he emailed to say that reading my piece gave him "that 'Roberta Flack' sensation—you were singing my life with your words. It is as if we were sitting on a sofa in 1974 listening together as it unfolded."

The whole episode was simply fun. Although it was a far cry from the Watergate investigation, it reminded me of how fortunate I've been to do all kinds of journalism over the years, from reviewing books and music to investigating government officials to supervising a big newsroom staff. With the Joni Mitchell essay, I once again was getting paid to report and observe, to think and communicate. Once again, I experienced the peculiar thrills of creativity under deadline. Like life itself, this assignment didn't go according to plan. Disappointments and unforeseen challenges forced me to go off-script. I had to scramble, improvise, and find another way. And it worked out pretty well. Against the odds, it gave me an unaccountable joy.

Acknowledgments

Writing a book is a solitary ordeal in many ways but, paradoxically, it's also a team effort. I'm deeply grateful to all of those at St. Martin's Press who helped along the way, especially my editor, Anna deVries, for her combination of sensitivity, knowledge, and mad skills. My wonderful agent, Pilar Queen, a force of nature, was always there to help. The cover design by Jonathan Bush not only perfectly captured my message but gave me great delight. The excellent Sujay Kumar, who fact-checked this manuscript, saved me from myself in several cases; whatever mistakes may remain are mine entirely. I benefited from the combined talents of my Macmillan team: Dori Weintraub in publicity and Danielle Prielipp in marketing, as well as Laura Clark in the publishers office. My former Duke student Maya Miller helped with research. I'm grateful to my early readers, including Joyce Pinchbeck Johnson (who not only wrote a classic memoir in the 1990s but was conveniently located in my Upper West Side apartment building), Brooke Kroeger, Brian Connolly, Neil Barsky, Linda Hirshman, Sophie Kleeman, and Betsey Higgins. For his invaluable technical help, I am indebted to Michael

Marissen. Thanks, too, to my supportive editors at *The Washington Post,* who understood when my column-writing fell off a bit, especially David Malitz, Liz Seymour, and Amy Argetsinger. I'm grateful to my brothers, David and Philip, who have provided guidance and wisdom from our Lackawanna days to the present, to their wonderful wives, Catherine and Maureen, and to their children—who are *almost* as dear to me as my own Grace and Alex. Finally, I am grateful to all the journalists whose work has inspired me over the decades: those I admired as an impressionable teenager; those I worked alongside in my forever newsroom, *The Buffalo News;* those I have known at *The New York Times*, *The Washington Post,* and elsewhere. Thank you for doing the work that is so necessary in helping our precious and fragile democracy to endure.